THE SUNDAY TIMES

KT-449-216

Learn while you earn

Everything you need to know about learning new skills while still earning money

Catherine Dawson

KoganPage

LONDON PHILADELPHIA NEW DELHI

Publisher's note

Every possible effort has been made to ensure that the information contained in this book is accurate at the time of going to press, and the publishers and authors cannot accept responsibility for any errors or omissions, however caused. No responsibility for loss or damage occasioned to any person acting, or refraining from action, as a result of the material in this publication can be accepted by the editor, the publisher or any of the authors.

First published in Great Britain in 2010 by Kogan Page Limited

Kogan Page Limited
120 Pentonville Road
London N1 9JN
United Kingdom
www.koganpage.com

British Library Cataloguing in Publication Data

A CIP record for this book is available from the British Library.

ISBN 978 0 7494 5898 0
E-ISBN 978 0 7494 5899 7

Typeset by Saxon Graphics Ltd, Derby
Printed and bound in Great Britain by MPG Books Ltd, Bodmin, Cornwall

So what is it all about?

The health sector is not just about doctors, nurses and physiotherapists, there are many other careers and jobs available.

In fact there are over 80 roles where apprenticeships are offered. Apprenticeships on offer can include clinical, administration, management, information technology, finance, estates (e.g. plumbing, engineering) and catering to name a few. Whilst most people associate the NHS with the health sector, increasingly healthcare is also provided across voluntary and independent organisations.

Do you know that?

- the NHS is the largest employer in England

- there are over 300 different jobs in the health sector

- there are a wide range of Apprenticeships across many occupations.

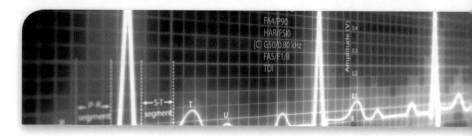

Career opportunities

The health sector offers a wide range of opportunities in numerous settings, providing an opportunity to develop skills in practical and technical areas as well as opportunities for career progression.

You could be working:

- in a community setting or in a hospital
- on a ward, in an office or in the grounds
- in the kitchen or in the lab, in contact with patients
- in a health authority office or working for a company that provides services to the NHS.

The NHS is very committed to developing its staff and providing opportunities for career progression. Healthcare delivery relies on team working, good communication, ethical and empathetic behaviour and well motivated staff. If you have these qualities then the healthcare sector could be for you!

There are a number of routes for all age groups by which you can become a young Apprentice from 14 to 16 years.

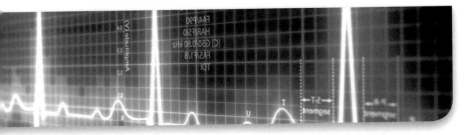

Apprenticeship

Apprenticeships are integrated workbased development programmes that reflect the application of knowledge and competences required of the modern day multi skilled workforce.

They lead to nationally accredited qualifications. Apprenticeships in the health sector are for everyone over 16 years of age and are available at two levels:

• Apprenticeships Level 2
• Advanced Apprenticeships Level 3

The key features to Apprenticeships are that you can work, learn and earn all at the same time.

Key components of Apprenticeships are:

• Employment Rights and Responsibilities (ERR)
• Technical Certificate
• Competency based qualification (NVQ)
• Key Skills

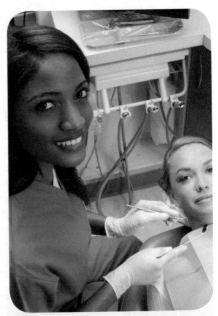

After my Apprenticeship?

In the NHS and wider health sector, learning never stops, there are always new things to learn.

After you have completed your Apprenticeship you may want to carry on learning from the career development opportunities available. There are a number of options for progression available to you, you may wish to:

• work while continuing your study
• complete more qualifications
• study for a foundation degree or a professional qualification
• go into full time study at university keep the job you are doing and continue to build up your experience.

Skills for Health

Take a look at the breadth of Apprenticeships available

- Health and Social Care
- Health (Blood Donor Support)
- Health (Clinical Support)
- Health (AHP Support - Physiotherapy and Occupational Therapy)
- Health (AHP Support - Speech and Language Therapy)
- Health (General Healthcare Support)
- Health (Decontamination)
- Health (Clinical Healthcare Skills)
- Health (Maternity / Paediatric Support)
- Health (Newborn Hearing Screening)
- Health (Obstetric Theatre Support)
- Health (Perioperative Care - Surgical Support)
- Support Services in Health Care
- Dental
- Pharmacy Technicians
- Business Administration
- Customer Services
- IT User and IT Services and Developments
- Marketing and Communications
- Events
- Management
- Payroll
- Contact Centres
- Accountancy
- Information and Library Services

- Electrical & Electronic Servicing
- Electrotechnical Engineering
- Engineering Construction
- Heating, Ventilation, Air Conditioning & Refrigeration
- Plumbing
- Maintenance Operations (Construction)
- Construction
- Procurement
- Purchasing and Supply
- Communications Technologies (Telecoms)
- Amenity Horticulture
- Hospitality and Catering
- Cleaning and Support Service Industry
- Photo Imaging
- Carry and Deliver Goods
- Driving goods vehicles
- Road Passenger Transport – Bus and Coach
- Traffic Office Vehicle Maintenance & Repair
- Transport Engineering and Maintenance Wholesale, Distribution, Warehousing and Storage
- Security Industry

Interested in becoming an Apprentice?

Check out your local vacancies on the National Vacancy Matching Service
http://www.apprenticeships.org.uk/Be-An-Apprentice/Vacancies.aspx

Skills for Health
www.skillsforhealth.org.uk/apprenticeships

NHS Careers to see the range of careers available in health
www.nhscareers.nhs.uk

Contents

Could you have a future in the...

ELECTRONIC SECURITY AND FIRE SYSTEMS INDUSTRY?

The private security industry continues to grow, so there has never been a better time to consider a career in this sector. **Skilled engineers** who can install and maintain security cameras, security and fire alarms and access control systems are in demand. The industry has opportunities for career progression, and many supervisors and managers started their careers as security installers.

The private security industry is an essential industry. It makes a key contribution to the UK economy and in protecting people against crime, terrorism and fire. Installing the equipment that is used to secure and monitor public and private areas is a skilled and vitally important job. One way of ensuring that the people working within the electronic security and fire systems industry are fully skilled is to train them through a formal apprenticeship scheme.

Employers range from large household-name companies to local independent installers.

WHAT'S INVOLVED?

As an Apprentice you will learn how to install and test security systems, repair faults and explain to customers how to use them. Security and fire systems installers fit and service electronic systems that detect intruders and control access to buildings or sites. They can also fit alarms in houses and business premises.

This particular apprenticeship programme is very hands-on and involves a considerable amount of practical skills in a variety of different working environments, so it's not all studying from books!

You could be installing security systems and rigging them to control panels, testing equipment, explaining to customers how to use the system and repairing faults. You will also be working with the latest technology in the form of wire-free systems, internet protocol or even biometric technology.

WHAT YOU WILL OBTAIN

An NVQ certificate, Key Skills certificate and Technical certificate. Advanced apprenticeships, with higher qualifications, are also available.

Expected Salary: £16,000 - £20,000*

HOW YOU CAN PROGRESS?

A career path within the electronic sector could include the following steps:

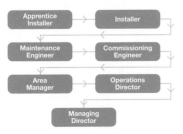

Many people start their own business after a few years experience.

WHAT TO DO NEXT?

If you are currently working within the security systems sector then you can approach your Manager to see if they will allow you to undertake the scheme. They can obtain further information about employing apprentices from Skills for Security, please call 08450 750 111 or visit **www.skillsforsecurity.org.uk.**

MORE INFORMATION

The British Security Industry Association (BSIA), represents employers in the security industry and Skills for Security is responsible for ensuring that the right skills and qualifications are developed .

To contact the BSIA, please call 0845 389 3889 or visit **www.bsia.co.uk**

If there is a particular company that you would like to work for, you can approach the recruitment manager of that organisation directly – again, refer them to Skills for Security, if they need information about how to set up an apprenticeship scheme.

If you are looking for a security company that employs apprentice engineers either of the above organizations may be able to help, or you can contact your local Connexions office (for people aged up to 19) or Jobcentre Plus.

> "I find it helps to have a practical side at the same time as studying at college because they both help each other out."
>
> Jemma Preston, Apprentice,
> Westmorland Fire & Security

> "I am thrilled at the opportunity of going to college to obtain a nationally recognised qualification and to help gain experience on how to fulfill my job criteria."
>
> Joe Swan-Liddell, Apprentice,
> Security Alarm Services

Introduction

As the credit crisis bites in the UK economy there is real concern from economists, politicians and members of the public about rising levels of unemployment, increasing debt and business failure. Recent research by the Trade Union Congress has found that jobseekers are now outnumbering vacancies by 20 to one and members of staff in Jobcentres have been warned that they need to be ready to respond to the tough times ahead.

In July 2009 the Office for National Statistics reported that the unemployment rate was 7.6 per cent for the three months to May 2009, up 0.9 per cent over the previous quarter and up 2.4 per cent over the year. This represents the largest quarterly increase in the unemployment rate since 1981. At the time of writing, unemployment stands at 2.38 million. Young people aged 16–24, in particular, have been hard hit with unemployment rising to a 16-year high of 726,000. As the recession deepens it is predicted that unemployment will exceed 3 million. This could have an adverse influence on consumer confidence, negatively affect high street spending and continue the downward spiral.

As a result of this economic crisis learner demand is buoyant. There is rising demand for full-time and part-time education and for work-based learning and training as people begin to fear for their job security and financial stability. In particular, there is demand for learning and earning opportunities that enable people to receive an income while they improve their skills and gain qualifications to improve their job prospects. Colleges and universities are experiencing a rapid rise in enquiries about part-time and vocational learning opportunities, and private training providers and employers are reporting an increased demand for all types of work-based learning and on-the-job training. Employment programmes that are available to help people to get into employment have seen a rising demand for places as employers cut back on jobs.

About this book

This book has been written in response to this demand for learning and earning opportunities. There is a wide variety of schemes available in all parts of the United Kingdom. However, it can be difficult to find information relevant to your specific circumstances and some schemes appear to be overly complicated with unclear eligibility criteria and obscure funding schemes. This book intends to address these problems by presenting all the schemes in an easily accessible format, providing information about the type of scheme, the amount of money available, eligibility criteria, application procedure, progression routes and further information if you would like to take part in any of the schemes described.

The book has been divided into four parts. Part I provides information about schemes for people who are interested in work-based learning, such as Apprenticeships or paid time off work for study. Part II provides information for people who are interested in study at further education colleges, perhaps on vocational courses that take place during the day or evening, or on block release. It describes the different schemes that are available and includes information about the qualifications that can be achieved. Part III goes on to look at the learning and earning opportunities that are available in the higher education sector, such as company sponsorship or vocational university courses that can be taken on a part-time basis. Part IV provides information for jobseekers and covers the various government schemes such as New Deal and entry-level programmes to help young people get into work. Appendix 1 provides case studies of people who have taken part in one of the schemes described in the book and Appendix 2 provides an overview of the funds that are available through the various schemes. The book concludes with useful organisations and websites for those of you who wish to take part in any of the schemes described in the book.

Finding the right scheme

Figures 1 to 4 will help you to find the scheme that is most suitable for you. The four charts cover England, Scotland, Wales and Northern Ireland. Work your way through the chart for the country in which you live, answering the questions until you are directed to the right scheme and the relevant chapter of this book.

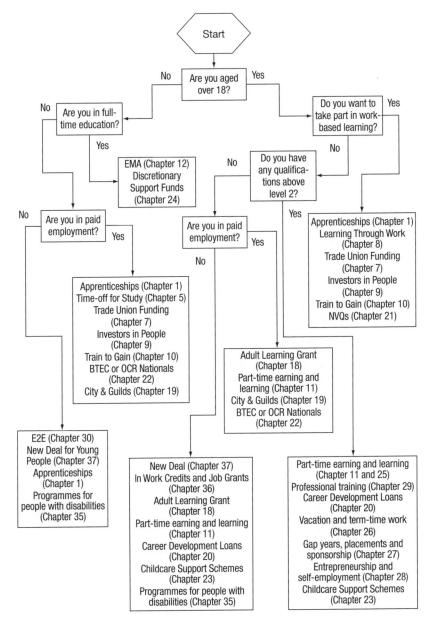

Figure 1. Finding the right scheme in England

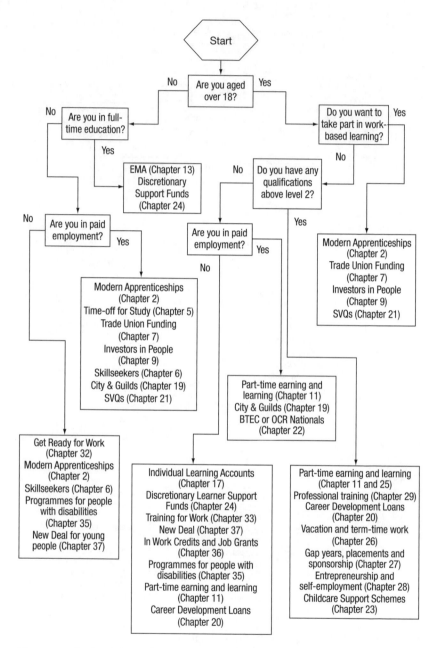

Figure 2. Finding the right scheme in Scotland

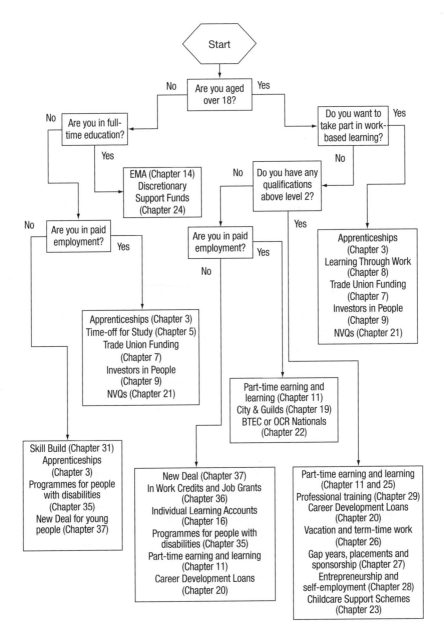

Figure 3. Finding the right scheme in Wales

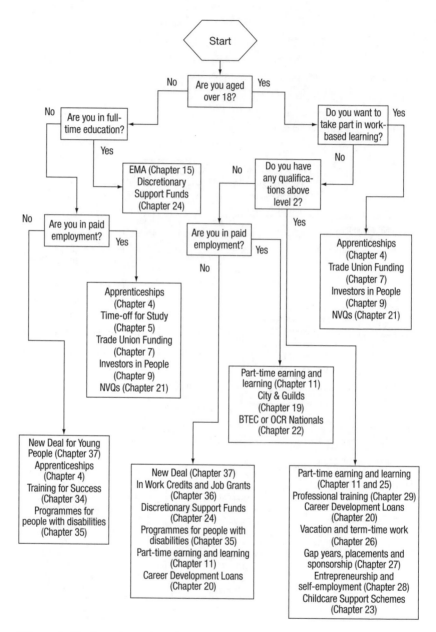

Figure 4. Finding the right scheme in Northern Ireland

I have worked within the education sector for over 25 years, and some of this time was spent conducting research with students who were seen to be 'non-traditional', that is students from poor backgrounds, mature students and those from a variety of minority ethnic groups. I have also undertaken research with jobseekers who are hoping to return to employment and with workers who are taking part in work-based learning schemes. Part of my research included an analysis of the financial barriers to participation in education, training and work-based learning and an assessment of what was required to overcome these barriers. I found that the main issues were lack of advice and information about financial matters and a lack of knowledge about the types of scheme that are available. People were unsure about where to find relevant information and lacked confidence in approaching learning providers direct.

This book will help to overcome these problems by providing all the information in one accessible, user-friendly source. This will help you to build your knowledge about what is available and increase your confidence so that you can approach learning providers or discuss work-based learning opportunities with your employer. I believe strongly that financial pressures should not be a barrier to participation in education and training, especially when it is possible to learn while you earn. There is a variety of schemes available and this book will help you to find the one that is most appropriate for your needs. I wish you every success in whichever learning and earning scheme you choose.

Part One
Learning and Earning in Employment

1 Apprenticeships (England)

If you live in England and wish to train in a specific job and earn a wage while you learn, you may be interested in the Apprenticeship scheme. There are different types of Apprenticeship available and these depend on your age, skills, interests, experience and the opportunities available in your area. At this present time there are around 130,000 businesses offering Apprenticeships in England in approximately 80 sectors of industry and commerce, according to the Learning and Skills Council (LSC). Recently, the Government has announced its intention to create 35,000 new Apprenticeship places so that all qualified young people will have a right to an Apprenticeship by 2013.

This chapter provides information about the types of Apprenticeship schemes available in England, advice about wages, eligibility criteria, applications procedures and possible progression routes, concluding with useful websites and telephone numbers for those who wish to find out more.

Type of scheme

There are different types of Apprenticeship available depending on your age, ability and preferences:

- Young Apprenticeships for people aged 14 to 16. These provide work experience in Years 10 and 11 of school.
- Programme Led Apprenticeships that provide the opportunity to begin your studies at college before you move onto an Apprenticeship with an employer. You may qualify for an Education Maintenance Allowance (EMA) of up to £30 a week with this type of scheme if you are between the ages of 16 and 18 (see Chapter 12).

- Apprenticeships for people aged 16 to 25. You cannot be in full-time education if you apply for this type of scheme. Apprenticeships at Level 2 (equivalent to five good GCSE passes) or Advanced Apprenticeships at Level 3 (equivalent to two A level passes) are available.
- Apprenticeships for people aged over 25. People who are already working, or those who are seeking work, can apply for this type of scheme. Apprenticeships at Level 2 or Advanced Apprenticeships at Level 3 are available.

Apprenticeships are available in a variety of jobs such as business administration, engineering, construction, care and community, public services, hospitality and management. Some Apprenticeships are more popular than others and some will not be available in all parts of the United Kingdom. To find out what Apprenticeships are available in your area you can telephone the National Apprenticeships helpline (details below) or visit the National Apprenticeship Service (NAS) website. Click on the 'Type of Apprenticeships' section to find out more about the types of jobs that are available (details below).

In general, Apprenticeships will take one to three years to complete, depending on the type of Apprenticeship, your specific needs and your rate of progress. At the start of your Apprenticeship you will be appointed a mentor who will work with your employer to make sure that the training is well planned. Once you have begun your Apprenticeship, your mentor will follow your progress and deal with any issues or problems that may arise. You will be treated the same as any other employee with the same employment rights. This means that you are entitled to at least 20 days' paid holiday per year as well as bank holidays. You also have the right to at least 24 hours free from work in a week or 48 hours free in two weeks. If you are under 18 this increases to 48 hours free from work in a week.

Qualifications

As an apprentice you work towards a National Vocational Qualification (NVQ) at Levels 2 or 3, Key Skills qualification and a technical certificate, such as a BTEC or City & Guilds (see Part II for more information about qualifications at further education level). It is also possible to work towards higher level qualifications through an Advanced or Higher Apprenticeship. At this present time Higher Apprenticeship programmes are available in the IT, engineering, purchasing and supply sectors. These enable apprentices to study for a foundation degree, learn new skills and earn a living at the same time (see progression routes, below). More information about learning and earning schemes in the higher education sector is provided in Part III of this book.

Amount of money

Wages vary depending on the type of Apprenticeship so you will need to discuss this with your potential employer, school or college. However, if you are undertaking an Apprenticeship with an employer you must receive a minimum of £95 a week (from August 2009) although many apprentices receive more than this amount. For example, a plumbing apprentice with a small company in the Midlands received £145.50 a week in his first year of training and will receive £165.50 a week in his second year of training (2008 and 2009 figures). In some sectors it is possible to receive up to £210 per week. Some employers will advertise a 'competitive salary' so you will need to discuss this amount with them before signing your contract (see job advertisement, in the box below).

Employers will offer other benefits, which could include gym membership, a company profit share scheme and a contributory pension scheme, so find out about these benefits when you consider how the wages compare with other jobs. Sometimes it may be worth considering a slightly lower paid Apprenticeship if the benefits and type of progression route suit your needs.

Eligibility criteria

To be eligible for an Apprenticeship you must be living in England (see Chapters 2, 3 and 4 if you live in other parts of the United Kingdom). You must not be in full-time education when you apply (except for Young Apprenticeships). There are no set entry requirements to do an Apprenticeship, although for some technical Apprenticeships you may need a GCSE at grade A* – C in English, maths and science (see job advertisement, below). Depending on your existing qualifications, skills and experience, you will be offered either an Apprenticeship or an Advanced Apprenticeship. In general, for an Advanced Apprenticeship you should have five GCSEs (grade C or above) or have completed an Apprenticeship. Some employers may request that you undertake additional literacy and/ or numeracy tests when you make your application.

To be eligible for a Young Apprenticeship you must be in Years 10 or 11 at school (usually when you are aged 14–16). Your school will need to have links with relevant employers; if it does not you could request that it sets up this type of link on your behalf.

Here is an example of the type of advertisement you can expect to see in local and national newspapers.

Engineering Design Apprenticeships

We are a leading international engineering company, with an excellent track record of Apprenticeship employment and progression. We are now beginning our annual recruitment to our well-established Apprenticeship programme.

You will be employed in one of our technical consultancy companies where you will be involved in a range of engineering design work. You will be provided with the opportunity to study on a day-release programme, studying towards a qualification such as an ONC/BTEC or HNC/Higher BTEC in Engineering. If you complete this successfully you will be given the opportunity to study for a degree at university.

These Apprenticeships provide an opportunity for you to take part in full-time employment while you train and are an excellent way to combine academic study with practical work experience in engineering.

You need to be 17 years or older and have a good standard of education, including maths and science subjects and an interest in engineering as a career. You need to be organised, with good time management skills and a willingness to learn and develop your abilities to a high level.

The remuneration package will include a competitive salary, 25 days' annual holiday plus relevant study leave, gym membership and a contributory pension scheme.

Contact us for an informal chat about these roles or you can apply in writing, including a copy of your CV. All interviews will be held in the local vicinity.

Application procedure

There are several ways to apply for an Apprenticeship. These opportunities tend to be advertised in your local Jobcentre or in the local newspaper (see job advertisement, above), or you could try approaching an employer direct. For this type of position you will need to complete an application form and/ or send your curriculum vitae (CV) with a covering letter. Comprehensive advice about producing a CV, including a useful 'CV builder' tool is available at http://careersadvice.direct.gov.uk/helpwithyourcareer/writecv.

Alternatively you can contact your local Learning and Skills Council (LSC) or Connexions service (if you are aged 13–19), which will put you in touch with a training provider that will then try to match you with an employer. Contact details of your local LSC can be obtained by clicking on the map available at www.lsc.gov.uk, and details of your local Connexions service can be obtained by clicking on the map available on the Connexions website (details below).

A third option is to search the 'vacancies' section on the NAS website (details below). Using this search facility you can find out what vacancies are available, view details and apply for the Apprenticeship. You will need to register to view the details of your search and to make an application.

Progression routes

There is a variety of progression routes available, depending on the type and level of Apprenticeship and your preferences, skills and ability. Some apprentices decide to stay with their employer and are offered a full-time position, with the possibility of further career progression within the company. Others decide to use their new skills and qualifications to apply for more advanced positions with a different employer.

It is also possible to use qualifications gained during an Apprenticeship to apply for further study, which could include Advanced Apprenticeships, Higher Apprenticeships, diplomas, foundation degrees, vocational degrees or other undergraduate degrees (see Part III). Indeed, the Government has recently announced its intention to enable Apprenticeships to count towards the UCAS tariff (this is the points system used by universities to assess the qualifications held by applicants when deciding whether they should be offered a place at university). This means that you would be able to use your qualifications gained during your Apprenticeship to apply for university study if this option should interest you at a later date.

Further information

Useful websites

www.apprenticeships.org.uk
This is the website of the National Apprenticeship Service, which was launched in April 2009. It contains all the information you need about Apprenticeships and has sections available for parents, employers and apprentices. You can use the online search facility to find a vacancy in your area and you can register an interest to receive more information about what is available. You can fill in the online form in the 'contact us' section of the website to receive a free DVD about Apprenticeships.

www.connexions-direct.com
This is the website of Connexions Direct, which provides information and advice for people aged 13–19. In the 'learning' section of this website you can read more about Apprenticeships. You can also find contact details of your local Connexions service, where staff will be able to provide information about vacancies in your area. They will also be able to offer advice about applying for an Apprenticeship.

http://careersadvice.direct.gov.uk
This website provides useful information about all aspects of jobs, careers and learning. You can use the tools on this site to assess your skills and interests and help you to produce a CV that can be used when you apply for an Apprenticeship. There is a useful discussion group that includes information about Apprenticeships.

www.jtltraining.com
JTL was formed in 1989 by the Electrical Contractors' Association (ECA) and the Electrical, Electronic and Plumbing Union (now Unite, the Union) to manage training in the electrical sector. JTL is a leading training provider to the building services engineering sectors, supporting up to 9,700 Apprenticeships in England and Wales.

On the website you can find useful information about the different types of Apprenticeship available in this sector, such as electrical, plumbing, heating and ventilation and engineering maintenance. The website helps you to understand whether this type of Apprenticeship is the right choice for you and, if so, you can download an application pack.

www.euskills.co.uk
This is the website of Energy and Utility Skills, which is the Sector Skills Council for the electricity, gas, waste management and water industries. Although Energy and Utility Skills does not recruit Apprentices it can provide you with useful information and advice about Apprenticeships within these industries. This includes information about the different types and level of Apprenticeship and useful links to employers that provide the jobs. There is a section on the website specifically for people from England.

Useful telephone numbers

National Apprenticeships helpline: 0800 015 0600.
Employers' Apprenticeships helpline: 0800 015 0400.
Connexions Direct: 08080 013 219 (for people aged 13–19).

2 Modern Apprenticeships (Scotland)

If you live in Scotland and wish to train in a specific job and earn a wage while you learn, you may be interested in the Modern Apprenticeship scheme. This enables anyone in Scotland, aged 16 and above, to achieve Scottish Vocational Qualifications (SVQ) at Level 3 or above, while working with an employer and receiving a wage. Modern Apprenticeships have been designed by employers, with their needs, and the needs of the apprentice, taken into account. They are supported by the Confederation of Business and Industry, the Trade Union Congress and a wide range of employers.

This chapter describes the scheme that is available in Scotland and provides information about the level of wages, the eligibility criteria, application procedures and progression routes, concluding with useful websites and contact numbers.

Type of scheme

Modern Apprenticeships are available in a wide variety of jobs at different levels, such as craft, technician and trainee management level. The amount of time spent on a Modern Apprenticeship varies, depending on the level of Apprenticeship, your skills, your previous qualifications and your personal experience. In general, they usually take between two and four years to complete. Modern Apprenticeships are made up of three parts:

1. An SVQ at Level 3. In certain cases you may be able to work towards a Level 2 qualification first, before embarking on the more advanced Level 3 qualifications. Some apprentices will be given the opportunity to progress to a Level 4 qualification. For further information about these qualifications and to understand more about the different levels available, visit www.sqa.org.uk.

2. Core skills development in communication, working with others, numeracy, information technology and problem solving.
3. Additional components that depend on the type of industry and your progress. For example, you may be able to study units from other SVQs, industry-specific qualifications or academic qualifications such as Higher National Certificates and Diplomas.

Apprenticeships are available in a wide variety of occupations, with the larger number being offered in the following career areas:

- construction;
- engineering;
- electro-technical;
- motor vehicle;
- management;
- health and social care;
- plumbing;
- business and administration;
- hospitality;
- early years care and education.

To obtain a list of how many Apprenticeships have been offered in previous years throughout Scotland in these career areas, visit www.mappit.org.uk.

Amount of money

Modern Apprentices are paid a wage, which, in most cases, is the going rate for that particular job. However, wages vary considerably, so you should discuss how much you will earn with your potential employer before signing your contract. To provide examples, using 2009 figures, a Modern Apprenticeship in Business and Administration at the University of Strathclyde will pay £165.55 per week in the first year and £198.65 per week in the second year. A Scottish Water apprentice will be paid approximately £10,500 a year, with progression to the next year's salary dependent on passing the relevant examinations and satisfactory progress in the workplace.

When considering how much you will be paid, you should also take into account other benefits that may be offered, especially if you intend to work for the company once you have completed your Apprenticeship. For example, some companies may offer additional annual paid holiday, life insurance cover, a generous occupational pension scheme, gym membership and a free nursery for the children of employees.

Eligibility criteria

The minimum age for entry is 16, with no upper age restriction. Although there are no specific entry qualifications required for a Modern Apprenticeship, some employers will specify certain grades in relevant subjects. Others may require you to take a literacy, numeracy and/or spatial awareness test (dependent on the type of job) as part of the application process. Also, your employer will need to be satisfied that you have the potential to complete your Apprenticeship successfully.

All apprentices will need to agree to an Individual Training Plan that covers the period of the Apprenticeship, prior to the commencement of training. This will identify and record your training needs and development as you enter and progress on your Apprenticeship.

Application procedure

You can obtain more information about applying for a Modern Apprenticeship from your careers adviser or guidance teacher, or you can contact your local Careers Scotland centre to discuss whether Modern Apprenticeships are suitable for your needs. You can find contact details of your local Careers Scotland centre by entering your postcode in the search facility available on the Careers Scotland website (details below).

If you are already in employment, talk to your employer to find out whether it already runs, or is interested in running, a Modern Apprenticeship scheme. (The majority of people are already with their employer when they decide to become an apprentice.) For some industries, such as construction and IT, recruitment takes place at specific times of the year, so you will need to find out when this is to make sure that you do not miss the deadline.

To access a list of Modern Apprenticeships throughout Scotland, visit www.mappit.org.uk. This website enables you to search for a vacancy alphabetically by job type. Information about the wages you can expect and the entry qualifications required are provided in each listing, along with contact details of the employer. If you are interested in a vacancy you can find out whether it is available and, if so, you can apply online. There is a simple application form to complete and a link to www.planitplus. net, which has a tool that enables you to produce your own CV that can be attached to your application. Closing dates for all vacancies are clearly displayed on the website.

Progression routes

Modern Apprenticeships have been designed to enable people to train on the job while receiving a wage. This is intended to create a 'responsive, motivated workforce by enabling them to develop their transferable skills through self-learning'. Many apprentices choose to stay with their employer on completion of their Apprenticeship, especially if a clear career progression plan has been developed (see case study, below).

Other apprentices use their new qualifications and skills to look for another position that will enable them to progress further in their chosen career and receive a higher wage. It is also possible for those apprentices who have enjoyed their learning and wish to take it further to progress to university study. More information about learning and earning schemes at higher education level is provided in Part III of this book.

Andrew undertook an Apprenticeship in Agricultural Engineering and now works as an Engineering Technician for the farming industry. Although he had enjoyed school he was not interested in staying on after he had completed his exams. This was because he wanted to earn a wage and was 'fed-up with the restrictions' that had been placed on him at school. Once he had reached the age of 17 he wanted to 'go out and earn a wage' rather than rely on his parents for money, even though his parents had hoped that he would go on to university and were willing to help him financially.

Initially, Andrew had obtained a job in a local garage, but was given 'boring jobs' that he didn't like. After a long conversation with his parents he was persuaded to visit a careers adviser. His parents had hoped that Andrew would be convinced to go to university, but instead he was told about Modern Apprenticeships. As he had grown up on a farm and had enjoyed helping his dad with 'all things mechanical', Andrew felt that he would really enjoy the Agricultural Engineering Apprenticeship. He was also tempted by the 'decent wage'. He applied for the post and had to attend a selection interview in which he was asked to undertake a numerical test and a practical exercise that Andrew found 'very easy and a bit insulting really'.

Andrew took two years to complete his Apprenticeship, studying one day a week at college and working the rest of the week on jobs such as repairing and maintaining equipment and helping to design and develop new machinery. Andrew felt that the work had helped him to work with other people and 'use new ideas to invent new things'. His parents said that they had been surprised at how challenging some of the work had been, and that it had kept Andrew 'interested and motivated'.

After completing his Apprenticeship, Andrew was offered a full-time position with the company. He now earns just over £19,000 a year and is happy in the work that he does. His parents admit that they are now pleased with what he has done, even though he didn't go to university. They acknowledge that his skills will be 'incredibly useful' when he inherits the farm.

Further information

Useful websites

www.scottish-enterprise.com/modern-apprenticeships
This site provides information about Modern Apprenticeships in Scotland. Click on the area of the map in which you live to be directed to the relevant information.

www.careers-scotland.org.uk
This is the website of Careers Scotland, which is part of Skills Development Scotland, Scotland's new skills body. On this site you can access the contact details of your local Careers Scotland agency. You can also find information about Modern Apprenticeships and access links containing information more specific to the area in which you live.

www.mappit.org.uk
This website contains detailed information about Modern Apprenticeships in Scotland. You can access an alphabetical database by job type of all the Modern Apprenticeships that are available, or that may become available in the future. Contact details of each position are provided, along with information about the type of job, what work you will be expected to do, the wage you will be paid and the type of qualifications you will gain. You can also access information about the personal qualities required for the position and the progression routes you can take upon completion.

www.planitplus.net
This website has been developed to help people of all ages find out about career and learning opportunities in Scotland. It has information on over 600 job profiles, which is useful if you want to find out more about specific jobs that may be available within the Modern Apprenticeship scheme.

www.euskills.co.uk
This is the website of Energy and Utility Skills, which is the Sector Skills Council for the electricity, gas, waste management and water industries. Although Energy and Utility Skills does not recruit Apprentices it can provide you with useful information and advice about Apprenticeships within these industries. This includes information about the different types of Apprenticeship and useful links to employers who provide the jobs. There is a section on the website specifically for people from Scotland.

Useful telephone numbers

Careers Scotland helpline: 0845 850 2502.
Helpline for employers to register a vacancy or find out more information about the Modern Apprenticeship promotion service: 0141 422 1070.

3 Apprenticeships (Wales)

If you live in Wales and wish to train in a specific job and earn a wage while you learn, you may be interested in becoming an apprentice. The Apprenticeship scheme enables you to undertake work-based learning with a local or national company while working towards a National Vocational Qualification (NVQ) and receiving a wage for your work. In Wales, Apprenticeships are managed and funded by the Welsh Assembly Government's Department for Children, Education, Lifelong Learning and Skills (DCELLS). At the beginning of 2009, the Welsh Assembly Government announced its intention to make a further £20 million available to help sustain and encourage new Apprenticeship recruitment.

This chapter describes the Apprenticeship schemes that are available in Wales and provides information about the level of wages, the eligibility criteria, application procedures and progression routes, concluding with useful websites and contact numbers.

Type of scheme

In Wales there are two types of Apprenticeship available. 1) Foundation Modern Apprenticeships (FMAs) are available for people who wish to study for a Level 2 NVQ. They are mainly open to people under the age of 18. An FMA can take up to two years to complete and may involve day or block release to a college or training centre. 2) Modern Apprenticeships tend to involve three or four years of training and lead to an NVQ Level 3. You may be required to attend a college or training centre for day or block release as part of your training. Some specialist Apprenticeships may require the training to take place at a specialist training centre that could be located at some distance from your home. However, the company for which you work will provide travel and living expenses if you have to undertake this type of training.

Both types of Apprenticeship are available in many career areas such as caring, engineering, business administration, office work, construction work, sport and recreation. To find out more about the different Apprenticeships that are available, visit the Careers Wales website (details below).

Amount of money

Apprentices who embark on an FMA will be paid a training allowance or wage of at least £50 a week. Apprentices who embark on a Modern Apprenticeship will be paid a wage equivalent to the going rate for that particular job. For example, an Aeronautical Engineering Apprenticeship based in Cardiff will be paid £8,200 per annum and a Catering Apprenticeship based in Cardiff will be paid the national minimum wage. (On 1 October 2009 the national minimum wage was set at £5.80 for adult workers aged 22 and over. The development rate for workers aged 18–21 inclusive was set at £4.83 an hour. If you are aged 16 or 17 the rate has been set at £3.57.)

Tom began work in September 2008 as an apprentice Gas Service Engineer. Before beginning his Apprenticeship he had worked on a building site as a 'general dogsbody', but he had been interested in the work undertaken by the gas engineers on site. He spoke to a few of the workers who told him to get in touch with 'CORGI-registered' employers in the local area. (CORGI is the UK's Confederation of Registered Gas Installers: registration with CORGI was a legal requirement for a business or self-employed person working on gas fittings or appliances. However, from April 2009 a new scheme called the Gas Safe Register replaced the CORGI gas registration scheme as Britain's gas safety authority. All engineers who carry out gas installation and related work will now need to be registered with the new Gas Safe Register scheme to continue trading legally. More information about this scheme can be obtained from www.gassaferegister.co.uk.)

Tom sent his CV to five different employers. Two said they were not taking on apprentices, one did not reply to his letter and two invited him for interview. Both of these employers offered Tom a job after the interview, but only one would enable him to undertake an Apprenticeship, so it was with this employer that Tom began his work and training. This was because Tom wanted to gain both qualifications and work experience, believing this would help him to progress in his future career. He also felt that the employer he chose was 'a bit more friendly' and would help to support Tom through his Apprenticeship.

Over the last six months Tom has spent his time 'learning the ropes' through helping to diagnose, find and replace problems in central heating systems, supervised by an experienced worker. He is working towards an NVQ Level 3 under the supervision of his employer, who is a qualified and experienced engineer. Most of his training takes place on the job, although he has attended a couple of gas safety training courses. Tom is receiving a salary of just under £11,000 a year, which is 'slightly more' than he received on the building site.

So far Tom has 'learnt quite a lot' about gas engineering. He is also improving his 'customer skills' because he has to meet new members of the public every day. He is keen to develop this area because he has always been 'a bit rubbish' at talking to people he does not know, but he knows that this will be an important part of the job, especially if he were to become self-employed at a later date.

After completing his Apprenticeship, Tom hopes to work with his current employer to 'gain more experience', before moving on to set up his own business. He believes that there is 'great demand' for gas service engineers in South Wales, and feels that there would be plenty of work if he were to go self-employed. However, he knows that he has to pass all his assessments and complete his Apprenticeship successfully before he can consider becoming self-employed.

Eligibility criteria

If you want to undertake an FMA, the qualifications you will need depend on the type of work you will undertake. Some may require you to possess GCSEs in subjects such as maths and English, and some employers may require you take an entrance test before you are offered a place.

If you are interested in a Modern Apprenticeship you will usually need four or five GCSEs at Grade C or above (or equivalent), although this may vary, depending on the type of Apprenticeship. Again, some employers will insist that you take an entrance test before you are offered a place. Some Apprenticeships are only open to people aged 16 to 24. However, if you are over this age and you wish to embark on an Apprenticeship, there are opportunities available that do not have any age restrictions. Contact Careers Wales as it will be able to offer advice about whether there are any Apprenticeships that are available for older workers in your area. If you have relevant work experience you will stand a better chance of being offered a position. Alternatively, you may be interested in the Individual Learning Account (Wales) scheme (see Chapter 16) or part-time learning opportunities at college (see Chapter 11) or at university (see Chapter 25).

Application procedure

To find out more information about the Apprenticeship vacancies that are available in your area, use the search facility available on the Careers Wales website (details below). Alternatively, you can contact your local careers centre or shop by telephone or e-mail. Addresses and contact numbers can be found in your local telephone directory or by visiting the Careers Wales website. If you prefer, you can visit the centre in person for Apprenticeship advice and information or to look at the vacancy boards for jobs and training.

Once you have found an Apprenticeship in which you are interested, you will need to complete an application form and/or produce a CV. Application forms can be obtained from Careers Wales or the company that is offering the Apprenticeship. Some of the larger companies enable you to download application forms from their website. A useful CV Wizard and CV Editor are available on the Careers Wales website, along with an Application Letter wizard. Some companies will request that you include a passport-size photograph with your application.

Progression routes

Apprentices who complete an FMA may decide to move on to a Modern Apprenticeship or go on to full-time employment, either with the same organisation or with a different company.

Apprentices who complete a Modern Apprenticeship may also choose to continue with full-time employment, again, with the same organisation or with a different employer, and some people decide to set themselves up in business when they have completed their Apprenticeship (see case study above). Alternatively, they may choose to continue their learning by studying for an HND, HNC, foundation degree or undergraduate degree. If you are interested in continuing your learning at higher education level, see Part III of this book for more information about the learning and earning schemes that are available.

Further information

Useful websites

www.careerswales.com
Careers Wales is funded by the Welsh Assembly Government and is available to give free careers information, advice and guidance to people of all ages in Wales. You can use the database on this site to hunt for an Apprenticeship in your area. Information is provided about the type of work that will be expected, the qualifications required and the wage you can expect to receive, along with contact details of the organisation offering the Apprenticeship. The service is available in English and Welsh.

www.jtltraining.com
JTL was formed in 1989 by the Electrical Contractors' Association (ECA) and the Electrical, Electronic and Plumbing Union (now Unite, the Union) to manage training in the electrical sector. JTL is a leading training provider to the building services engineering sectors, supporting up to 9,700 Apprenticeships in England and Wales.

On this website you can find useful information about the different types of Apprenticeship available in this sector, such as electrical, plumbing, heating and ventilation and engineering maintenance. The website helps you to understand whether this type of Apprenticeship is the right choice for you, and if so, enables you to download an application pack.

www.euskills.co.uk
This is the website of Energy and Utility Skills, which is the Sector Skills Council for the electricity, gas, waste management and water industries.

Although Energy and Utility Skills does not recruit Apprentices it can provide you with useful information and advice about Apprenticeships within these industries. This includes information about the different types and level of Apprenticeship and useful links to employers who provide the jobs. There is a section on the website specifically for people from Wales.

Useful telephone numbers

Learning and Careers Advice in Wales: 0800 100 900.

4 Apprenticeships (Northern Ireland)

If you live in Northern Ireland and wish to train in a specific job and earn a wage while you learn, you may be interested in becoming an apprentice. In Northern Ireland Apprenticeships are delivered jointly by employers and training suppliers to enable you to undertake training, build your knowledge and skills, gain nationally recognised qualifications (including NVQs and technical certificates) and receive a wage from the day you begin your Apprenticeship.

This chapter describes the Apprenticeship schemes that are available in Northern Ireland and provides information about the level of wages, the eligibility criteria, application procedures and progression routes, concluding with useful websites and contact numbers.

Type of scheme

In Northern Ireland there are two types of Apprenticeship: Level 2 Apprenticeships enable you to study for a Level 2 qualification, usually over a two-year period; and Level 3 Apprenticeships enable you to study for a Level 3 qualification, usually over a three- or four-year period.

Both levels of Apprenticeship are available in a variety of areas, such as information technology, mechanical engineering, joinery, plumbing, travel services and beauty therapy. Visit the Department for Employment and Learning in Northern Ireland (DELNI) website for specific information about all the different Apprenticeships that are available (details below). To find out more about the different levels of qualification and how they compare with other types of qualification, visit www.qcda.gov.uk.

A Pre-Apprenticeship scheme is available for people who are not in employment or full-time education (usually for those aged 16–18). This scheme is for young people who have been assessed as being capable of achieving a Vocationally Relevant Qualification (VRQ) at Level 2, but who have not obtained a job. It provides the opportunity for young people to progress into employment through the Apprenticeship route. Pre-Apprenticeships are offered as part of the Training for Success scheme and are discussed in more detail in Chapter 34.

Skillsafe

In May 2009 the Minister for Employment and Learning in Northern Ireland announced measures to assist apprentices within the manufacturing engineering sector who have been placed on short-time working. The scheme is called 'Skillsafe' and provides extra help to affected apprentices through additional training that will count towards their Apprenticeship. A training allowance will be paid to those apprentices experiencing a reduction in their wages due to their short-time working. It is hoped that this scheme will be expanded to cover other sectors that may be affected by the recession. More information about the scheme can be obtained from the DELNI (details below).

Amount of money

As an apprentice you will be paid the going rate for the job. However, rates of pay vary depending on the company you will be working for and the type of Apprenticeship that you undertake. For example, the Engineering Training Council (details below) points out that, for engineering Apprenticeships, companies currently on the programme have a starting wage of between £85 and £220 per week. This figure increases each year of the Apprenticeship. Contact your chosen employer before you make your application to check that you are happy with the salary level. You should also find out about other benefits and perks that may be included, such as a pension scheme, gym membership, a nursery for the children of employees and relocation allowances.

Eligibility criteria

To be eligible to apply for an Apprenticeship you must be resident in Northern Ireland. Individual Apprenticeship suppliers set their own entry criteria, which may include GCSEs in English and maths, and a technical subject for some specialist Apprenticeships at Level 3 stage. Other employers will ask you to complete an entry test prior to, or during, your interview. Apprenticeships in Northern Ireland are available for people of all ages, and to both existing and newly recruited employees.

Here is an example of the type of advertisement you can expect to see in local and national newspapers.

Apprenticeship in Countryside Management

Are you interested in an Apprenticeship in Countryside Management? Looking for a job with a difference, outdoors? We are currently seeking apprentices for a number of roles within the countryside. These are exciting opportunities to gain valuable practical experience alongside our highly experienced staff on a variety of projects.

You will be given the chance to undertake a wide range of vocational training including NVQs, Key Skills and First Aid. This training will be provided in partnership with local training centres and further education colleges. Suitable candidates must be physically fit, showing a strong commitment and desire to move forward in countryside management. You should display a willingness to learn and be committed to take part in a year-long placement.

More information about the Apprenticeships and application forms can be obtained from our recruitment line. Selection will be by interview and aptitude test.

Application procedure

To find out what apprenticeships are available in Northern Ireland, use the ApprenticeshipsNI Supplier Map available on the DELNI website (details below). The easiest way to find the map is to type 'ApprenticeshipsNI Supplier Map' into the search box on the home page, and you will find all the Apprenticeship suppliers in Northern Ireland. Click on the area in which you are interested and download the list of suppliers, where you will find contact details, including e-mail addresses. You can contact these organisations direct to find out what opportunities are available in your area and to request an application form.

Alternatively, you can visit the Careers Service Northern Ireland website (details below) for more information about Apprenticeships. On this website you can click on the map to find contact details of your local careers adviser, which you can contact by telephone or e-mail, or visit them in person for advice and guidance.

Once you have found a suitable Apprenticeship in your chosen career area you will have to make sure that you satisfy the entry criteria that have been set by the employer. This could be GCSEs or equivalent, or may involve an examination or aptitude test and interview (see job advertisement above).

Progression routes

Apprentices who have successfully completed their Level 2 Apprenticeship can move onto the next level, if a suitable position is available. Alternatively, they might decide to continue with their present employer or apply for a new job with a different one.

Apprentices who have successfully completed their Level 3 Apprenticeship may decide to continue their learning, whether full-time or part-time at college or university. If you are interested in study at further education level, more information about learning and earning schemes is provided in Part II of this book. If you are interested in studying at higher education level, more information is provided in Part III. Alternatively, you may decide to continue working with your current employer, apply for a new position with a different company or establish your own business.

Further information

Useful websites

www.delni.gov.uk/apprenticeshipsni
This is the website of the Department for Employment and Learning in Northern Ireland. On this site you can find more information about Apprenticeships, with different sections available for apprentices, employers and

training suppliers. You can access a map of Apprenticeship suppliers and download Level 2 and Level 3 Apprenticeships Frameworks. These provide detailed information about what is included in each Apprenticeship.

www.careersserviceni.com
The Careers Service Northern Ireland has been developed to offer advice and guidance on learning, training and employment opportunities in Northern Ireland. The website contains contact details of careers services throughout Northern Ireland, along with comprehensive advice about writing a CV and covering letter. There are also useful tips about filling in application forms and attending a job interview.

www.etcni.org.uk
The Engineering Training Council (ETC) is an employer-led body, governed by a council whose members are elected to ensure a broad representation of the engineering community in Northern Ireland. It is dedicated to supporting the engineering industry by coordinating training and learning opportunities for new entrants and the existing workforce. On the website you can find further information about the Engineering Apprenticeships that are available, including lists of employers, job descriptions and the skills and qualifications that are required. You can download an application pack or fill in the online form if you are interested in applying for an Apprenticeship.

www.euskills.co.uk
This is the website of Energy and Utility Skills, which is the Sector Skills Council for the electricity, gas, waste management and water industries. Although Energy and Utility Skills does not recruit Apprentices it can provide you with useful information and advice about Apprenticeships within these industries. This includes information about the different types and level of Apprenticeship and useful links to employers that provide the jobs. There is a section on the website specifically for people from Northern Ireland.

Useful organisations

Skillsafe

If you are an apprentice in Northern Ireland and you have been affected by the economic downturn through a reduction in wages and reduced working hours, the Skillsafe scheme may be able to help. More information about this scheme can be obtained from the following address:

Department for Employment and Learning
Lesley Buildings, 61 Fountain Street, Belfast BT1 5EX
Tel: (028) 9044 1880; e-mail: skillsafeni@delni.gov.uk;
website: www.nidirect.gov.uk/skillsafeni

Useful telephone numbers

For information about Apprenticeships in Northern Ireland contact: 0800 0854 573 (Monday to Friday, 9:00 am to 5:00 pm); Text phone (for use by deaf people or those with communication difficulties): 0800 3280 824. The Careers Service Support Unit can be contacted on 028 9044 1781.

5 Time off for Study or Training

This scheme is aimed at people aged 16–17 who are in paid employment and wish to improve their skills. It is available in all parts of the United Kingdom and has been designed to help improve the skills and qualifications of young people who have entered jobs that offer little education and training. The scheme enables you to gain new skills and achieve a nationally recognised qualification that will be of personal benefit in the future.

This chapter describes the Time off for Study or Training (TfST) programme and provides information about the level of wages, the eligibility criteria, application procedures and progression routes, concluding with useful websites and contact numbers.

Type of scheme

This scheme provides the opportunity for young people in employment to take paid time off from their work to improve their skills and qualifications at Level 2. Although you will be working towards Level 2 qualifications, you do not have to start at that level, but can instead work your way up, beginning with Level 1 or below if it is more appropriate for your needs. To find out more about the different levels of qualifications that are available, and to see how your existing qualifications compare with other qualifications, visit the Qualifications and Curriculum Development Agency (QCDA) website (details below).

You are expected to work towards a 'relevant' qualification. This means that it would be relevant to you, rather than to your employer, so as long as it will enhance your employment prospects and help you to improve your qualifications, it does not have to relate specifically to your current job. For example, you might find it useful to improve your qualifications in maths and English, rather than study a craft that is related specifically to your work (see the case study below). Examples of the type of qualifications that you can study towards include:

- NVQs at Level 2;
- BTEC First Certificates or Diplomas;
- City & Guilds qualifications at Intermediate level;
- GCSEs.

The amount of time that you can have off work depends on the course requirements and the needs of your employer and the business. You will need to discuss this with your employer and reach an agreement with which you are both happy (see the case study below). Your employer must give you a 'reasonable' time off work, and, although there are no set limits as to what constitutes 'reasonable', it is taken to mean around one day a week, depending on your course and your needs.

Training can take place as day or block release at a local college, with another employer or training provider, or in your current workplace. It is also possible to undertake the training through open or distance learning, which can include online learning.

Yeah, I work on the Granby (the local industrial estate)... been there since last year when I done with school... learning to be a CNC turner. So I do training and that on the job... it was me boss, he said where's your maths and English. I never done them at school, see... he said I should do 'em and he would pay, like, and let me have time off, like, away from here on Fridays. So now I'm doing them down there (at the local further education college). If I get them qualifications and I've done the work, you know, experience and all that, I'll get 22,000 a year. Geoff who I work with is on that much. So get me maths and English... It's alright down there, not like school and Geoff's on that much, it's like worth it. *Jerrell, 17, Weymouth*

Amount of money

You are entitled to receive payment for your time off at the appropriate hourly rate. This is usually worked out by dividing the amount of a week's pay by the number of your normal working hours in the week. If your employer refuses to permit time off, or unreasonably withholds your pay, you can make a complaint to an employment tribunal. If you need to do this you should seek advice from your local Citizen's Advice Bureau (CAB). You can find your local CAB by entering your postcode in the box on the home page of www.citizensadvice.org.uk, or you can visit www. adviceguide.org.uk for further information and advice.

Eligibility criteria

The scheme is open to non-disabled and disabled young people (it should not affect your right to disability benefits, but you should check that this is the case with the course provider and your Jobcentre Plus prior to enrolment). Participants have to be aged 16–17, although anyone who turns 18 while on the programme is able to finish their course.

To be eligible for the scheme you must not be receiving any full-time secondary or further education and have not achieved a certain standard of education and training. This is usually taken to be any qualification from Level 2 or above, such as five GCSEs at grade A – C or an NVQ at Level 2. You cannot take part in this scheme if you are self-employed or in the Armed Services.

Employers cannot refuse to allow you time off from work, even if you have not worked for the company for very long, or if you only work a limited number of hours a week, or if you work for a small business.

Application procedure

If you are interested in this scheme you should discuss the issue with your employer. If they do not know about the scheme you can direct them to a leaflet called *Time off for Study or Training: A guide for employers*, which can be downloaded from http://publications.teachernet.gov.uk.

You should also seek some careers advice to find out what courses and qualifications may be suitable for your needs. You can do this by speaking to an adviser at your local Connexions service (details of your local Connexions service can be found by clicking on the map available at www.connexions-direct.com). Alternatively, you can seek advice from Connexions Direct, Learndirect Scotland (if you live in Scotland) and the careers service by telephoning the numbers listed below.

If you hope to attend a course at your local college you can request a prospectus or search for a course online. Alternatively, you may prefer to visit the college in person where you will be able to speak to an adviser. Most colleges will require you to complete a simple application form and then you will be given details about how to enrol. During the enrolment session you should be given the opportunity to speak to course tutors so that you can check that the course is suitable for your needs prior to enrolment. Private training providers and other employers may require you to attend an interview in addition to completing an application form. More information about studying at further education level and the type of qualifications that are available is provided in Part II of this book.

Progression routes

This scheme has been set up as part of a wider strategy to ensure that more young people stay on in education until they reach the age of 19. If you enjoy your learning you may decide to continue with it by enrolling on a full-time course at a college of further education. Indeed, some people find that they enjoy their learning so much they that decide to study for a Foundation Degree with a view to entering university. More information about learning at further education level is provided in Part II of this book and more on learning at higher education level is provided in Part III.

However, most people who take part in this type of scheme use their new qualifications to improve their employment prospects, perhaps through obtaining promotion in their current job, or by applying for a new job in which they can utilise their new qualifications. Other people who have gained their qualifications decide to move on to an Apprenticeship (see Chapters 1, 2, 3 and 4 for more information about Apprenticeships in each part of the United Kingdom).

Further information

Useful websites

www.delni.gov.uk
A leaflet called *ER26 Time off for Study and Training* can be downloaded from this site. It provides more information about the scheme for employers and employees who live in Northern Ireland.

www.connexions-direct.com
Connexions is a service that offers advice and guidance to young people. Type 'time off for study or training' into the search box on the home page and you will be able to find out more about the scheme.

www.careers-scotland.org.uk
If you live in Scotland you can obtain more information and advice about the Time off for Study or Training scheme by contacting Careers Scotland.

www.qcda.gov.uk
This is the website of the Qualifications and Curriculum Development Agency (QCDA), which is a new organisation being developed from the Qualifications and Curriculum Authority. On this site you can find more information about the different types of qualification that are available and how these compare with each other.

Useful telephone numbers

A Connexions Direct adviser can be contacted on 080 8001 3219. If you prefer to text you can do so on 07766 413 219. If you have hearing difficulties you can textphone on 08000 968 336.
Careers Advice Service (England): 0800 100 900.
Learndirect Scotland helpline: 0808 100 1855.

6 Skillseekers (Scotland)

The Skillseekers programme is available to people aged 16–19 living in Scotland who wish to develop their skills and improve their qualifications. It is open to young people who are no longer in full-time education at school or college and is available both for people who are already in work and those who are seeking work. At the time of writing this scheme is still in existence. However, the Scottish Government has indicated recently that the Skillseekers programme will be phased out in Scotland as the Modern Apprenticeship programme is extended to S/NVQ Level 2 (see Chapter 2 for more information about Modern Apprenticeships in Scotland).

This chapter describes the existing Skillseekers programme in Scotland and provides information about the level of wages, the eligibility criteria, application procedures and progression routes, concluding with useful websites and contact numbers.

Type of scheme

There are two types of scheme available through the Skillseekers programme. Skillseekers for trainees is available for young people who have left full-time education who are seeking a job. With this scheme you will have the opportunity to gain work experience, improve your qualifications, develop new skills and obtain references that will help you to apply for a job. You will also receive extra help with activities related to job-hunting, such as attending interviews, writing letters, literacy, numeracy and confidence building.

Skillseekers for employees is available for young people who are already in a job who wish to improve their skills and qualifications. In general, it tends to be your employer who organises the training, often with the help of a training company or college. You will need to agree a training plan, which will give details of the qualifications that you are working towards and information about how long your training will last.

This can be up to two years, depending on the type of course and your skills and abilities.

Skillseekers in Scotland (employees and trainees) work towards Scottish Vocational Qualifications (SVQ) or National Vocational Qualifications (NVQs). These include the following levels and you can start at, and progress to, a level that suits you:

Level 1: foundation and basic work activities;
Level 2: a broad range of skills and responsibilities;
Level 3: Craft/Technician/Apprenticeship.

Vocational Qualifications (VQs) are a measure of the skills and knowledge you have developed in doing the job itself and are recognised and accepted by industry throughout the United Kingdom. They are assessed practically (on your ability to do the job either at the college or training centre, or in your workplace) and not based on your ability to pass examinations. More information about SVQs can be obtained from www.sqa.org.uk and more information about NVQs from www.qcda.gov.uk.

Types of employment

Skillseekers aims to match the training needs of young people more closely with the skill requirements of local employers, and at the same time offers young people the means to take more responsibility for their choice of training and job/career. This means that there is a wide range of opportunities available through Skillseekers, including the following:

- business administration;
- engineering maintenance;
- engineering – fabrication and welding;
- hairdressing;
- health and social care (residential care);
- heavy vehicle mechanics;
- light vehicle mechanics;
- plumbing;
- professional cookery;
- science lab technicians.

To find out what opportunities are available in the area in which you live, speak to your guidance teacher at school or a careers adviser from Careers Scotland (details below).

Amount of money

If you are a non-employed trainee you will be paid a minimum of £55 per week (2009 figures). If you are an employed Skillseeker you will be paid the usual rate that you are paid for your job by your employer (see case study below).

Maxine had not studied for any exams at school because she had contracted meningitis when she was 15. Having had more than a year off school, and having gained no qualifications, her careers adviser had suggested that she enrol on the Skillseekers programme because it would enable her to improve her skills and gain qualifications and work experience that would improve her chances of obtaining a job. Her parents encouraged her to take part in the scheme because they felt that she was a 'clever girl' who had lost out through no fault of her own. They felt that she would be able to gain the required qualifications easily, and that she would not have 'any problem finding work'.

At college Maxine obtained her European Computer Driving Licence (ECDL) and studied other IT courses, along with gaining maths and English qualifications. She was paid a training allowance while she studied. Maxine found the money 'very useful' because it enabled her to go out with her friends who were all working, and she could buy clothes for her work experience and job interviews.

After having studied for a year at college, Maxine obtained a job with a local company, where she was able to study towards a Level 3 qualification in business administration, while being paid a wage. She progressed onto a Modern Apprenticeship with the same company, and has now obtained a full-time, permanent administrative position, for which she is earning just under £18,000 a year.

Eligibility criteria

Skillseekers is available for people living in Scotland aged 16–19, although in certain circumstances it may be possible for people up to the age of 25 to take part in the scheme. If you are older than 19 contact Careers Scotland for information specific to your circumstances.

The scheme is available for people in work and those who are looking for work, but you must not be taking part in any full-time education at school, college or university.

Application procedure

To find out more about Skillseekers, contact your local Careers Scotland centre. You can find your nearest centre by telephoning 0845 8502 502 or by entering your postcode in the location facility on the Careers Scotland website (details below).

If you do not already have a job a personal careers adviser will put you in touch with a training company that will arrange a placement with a suitable employer and organise your training. The careers adviser can also help you to find a work placement.

You will need to fill in a short application form, which will ask for your personal details, previous qualifications (if any), previous work experience (if any), your hobbies and interests, other relevant skills and experience and contact details of two referees who are able to provide a reference for you. This could be a teacher or an employer, for example. If your application is successful you will need to attend an interview with prospective employers. Tips for attending interviews can be obtained from the Careers Scotland website (details below).

If you already have a job, speak to your employer who will be able to work with a college or training provider to organise a training plan for you. You will not have to attend an interview, as you are already in employment. Depending on the type of course you undertake, you may have to fill in a short application form, which will be available from the training provider, and you will need to enrol on the course. If your employer is unwilling to train you to at least Level 2, you may have to think about other types of employment, or consider other training opportunities, such as the Time off for Study and Training scheme (see Chapter 5) or part-time learning opportunities (see Chapter 11).

Progression routes

Many people move onto a Modern Apprenticeship after Skillseekers. These are available in a wide variety of industries and provide the opportunity to continue with your learning while earning a wage (see Chapter 2). Some people who have not got a job before they begin with Skillseekers find that they are able to secure a job, or an Apprenticeship, with employers for whom they have worked during their work placement on the programme (see case study above).

If you enjoy your learning and wish to take it further, it is possible to use your VQs as an alternative to academic entry qualifications to gain a full-time college place. More information about study at further education level is provided in Part II of this book.

Further information

Useful websites

www.careers-scotland.org.uk
This is the website of Careers Scotland, which is part of Skills Development Scotland, Scotland's new skills body. On this site you can access contact details of your local Careers Scotland agency and find more information about the Skillseekers programme. You can also find information about Modern Apprenticeships and access links containing information relevant to the area in which you live. The site contains useful information about applying for jobs and attending interviews, including an 'interview game' to guide you through your preparation for an interview.

Useful telephone numbers

Careers Scotland helpline: 0845 850 2502.

7 Trade Union Funding

If you are in paid employment and you are a member of a trade union or a union representative or officer, you may be able to receive subsidised or free education and training while you are earning a wage. All representatives or union officers have the legal right to reasonable paid time off during working hours for trade union duties, which includes training (if your employer recognises the union for collective bargaining). If you are an ordinary member of a union you should be entitled to some paid time off work if you do not have any qualifications above Level 2, and some employers will enable you to take paid time off for qualifications above this level, especially if the qualification is work-related.

This chapter discusses the larger trade unions that provide funding and includes information about the level of funding, the eligibility criteria, application procedures and progression routes, concluding with useful addresses, contact numbers, useful websites and further reading. If your trade union is not covered in this chapter, contact your local union representative for information about the education and training schemes that are available for members.

Type of scheme

In 1998 the Government set up the Union Learning Fund (ULF) as a source of funding available for trade unions to help them promote and organise learning opportunities for their members. For more information about this scheme, visit www.unionlearningfund.org.uk. There are different schemes run by trade unions, some of which are supported by the ULF. Some of these may provide free education and training for their members, or for union representatives and officers. Others provide small grants for their members to enrol on various types of education programme. The schemes of the largest unions in the United Kingdom are listed below.

The Communication Workers Union (CWU)

The CWU represents the communications industry, which includes members in postal, administrative, financial and telephone companies throughout the United Kingdom. The CWU Education and Training Department has been set up to help encourage and promote education and training amongst members and union representatives. There are two main strands to this work: activist education and training and lifelong learning activities. Courses currently being delivered in the lifelong learning section include IT, English and maths refreshers, communication skills, English for Speakers of Other Languages (ESOL), British Sign Language and conversational Spanish. CWU courses are offered to members at greatly discounted prices and are sometimes free of charge. More information about the courses can be obtained from your union representative or from the CWU (details below).

The General Federation of Trade Unions (GFTU)

This GFTU is the federation for specialist unions. Affiliated unions cover a wide range of jobs and industries from clothing and textiles to youth services, from ceramics and pottery to probation services. A full range of courses is offered through the Educational Trust, aimed at union members, union representatives and union officers. These include courses in industrial relations, health and safety, information technology and equality and diversity, which are held in different venues around the country. All the courses are accredited through the Open College Network (OCN) and all students who take part have the opportunity to gain a qualification for their studies. More information about the OCN can be obtained from www.nocn.org.uk. The Trust also awards grants and prizes to students. Details of all these schemes can be obtained from your union representative or direct from the GFTU (details below).

The GMB

The GMB was originally known as the General Municipal Boilermakers, but is now simply known as the GMB. It is a general union covering a variety of trades and the service and production sectors. The GMB promotes and supports the education and training of officers, representatives and members. Each region has its own Regional Education Officer who will be able to offer advice and guidance about the opportunities available. Contact details can be found on the GMB website (details below).

The National Union of Rail, Maritime and Transport Workers (RMT)

The RMT represents members in almost every sector of the transport industry, from mainline and underground rail to shipping and offshore, buses and road-freight. RMT Learning provides information, advice and guidance for workers who are interested in taking part in education and training, through a network of development workers for London, the South, the North, Network Rail and Shipping. The development workers are able to liaise with learning providers and arrange for time off work to be taken. They can also help members through setting up seminars on issues such as money management and pension rights. For a list of development workers and learning contacts within the RMT, contact the union direct (details below).

The Union of Construction, Allied Trades and Technicians (UCATT)

UCATT represents construction workers and related trades throughout the United Kingdom. It has created a range of education and training services to benefit individual and potential members, including a number of training centres that offer a wide variety of courses to members. Through the education and training section a series of programmes have been introduced to help the construction workforce become more skilled, and to be able to achieve qualifications to prove their ability and help them to progress within the industry. More information about the types of courses available and the qualifications that can be achieved can be obtained from the union or from your local learning representative (details below).

Unison

Unison represents the rights of public sector workers across the United Kingdom. It has a Learning and Organising Service that coordinates education and training for activists and members. This includes courses in areas such as accounting, committee administration, counselling and care skills, health and social care and marketing. Regional education officers and life-long learning advisers can help members to access education opportunities and will be able to provide advice on financial support for education and training. You can download an information leaflet called a *Guide to Courses for Members and Activists* from its website (details below).

Unite

Unite was formed by a merger between two of Britain's leading unions, the T&G and Amicus. It has trained Union Learning Representatives available to offer advice and guidance to members and colleagues in the workplace about the range of learning and training opportunities available through the union. This includes areas such as industrial relations, health and safety and equality and diversity. Unite also offers bursaries to members who wish to improve their skills and qualifications. For information about courses and bursaries speak to your Union Learning Representative or visit the Unite website (details below).

Over the years I have carried out a number of focus groups with adult learners who are undertaking courses that have been set up by their union. Some of the adults were on courses that were training them to become efficient and effective union representatives, whereas others were on courses of their choosing that had been paid for by their trade union. The feedback is always extremely positive, with learners having enjoyed, and benefitted from, their course. Many choose to continue their learning by enrolling on other courses and taking part in more advanced study.

The courses for which I undertake focus group evaluations are provided by adult residential colleges, which specialise in offering both short- and long-term courses for adults in a supportive, residential environment. Short courses tend to be offered over a period of two days to a week. There is a wide range of short course subjects on offer and these vary between colleges: some specialise in arts subjects, others in social and community issues, others in information technology. Some colleges offer free accommodation and meals to students who are attending short courses. In these colleges students learn from the tutors and from each other: living at the college is seen to be part of the learning experience.

Long courses can lead to diplomas, foundation degrees or the first year of an undergraduate degree. Most colleges define adults as over the age of 21 and some will not offer places on their long courses to anyone who has already obtained higher education qualifications. The colleges have made arrangements with local universities to offer a number of degree course places for those having successfully completed their course at the residential college. Accommodation, meals and childcare are provided free of charge at the residential colleges and there is a bursary available for adults who wish to study on these long courses. More information about these bursaries can be obtained from *The Essential Guide to Paying for University* (details below).

If you are interested in finding out more about courses offered by adult residential colleges, contact details of the residential colleges are listed below, or you can visit the Adult Residential Colleges Association website for more information: www.arca.uk.net. *Catherine Dawson, 2009*

Amount of money

The amount of money you could receive depends on the scheme, the union to which you belong, the type of learning you wish to undertake and whether you are a union member or a union representative or officer. Union representatives will be able to receive free training and expenses associated with that training. Union members may be able to receive a small grant towards their learning costs. For example, Unite offers its members who wish to undertake a course at higher education level a payment of up to £800, depending on the length of course, and for vocational applicants up to £400 per course. Other unions provide courses for members that are free or heavily discounted.

Eligibility criteria

Grants, bursaries and subsidised training are only available to union members and/or union representatives and officers. To qualify you will need to have been a member for a specified length of time, have no subscription arrears and continue to pay all membership subscriptions throughout the time of your course.

Individual unions may set additional eligibility criteria, such as placing a limit on the number and level of qualifications already held by the applicant. Check with your union representative for more information.

Application procedure

In the first instance you should contact your union representative to find out what schemes are offered by your union. If relevant, they will put you in touch with the education/learning department of the union who will be able to offer more advice about what is available and let you know whether you qualify for the scheme. If you prefer, you can contact the education/learning department direct by using the contact details provided at the end of this chapter. Alternatively, you can visit the unionlearn website for independent advice or to search their course database (details below).

If you find a course in which you are interested, in most cases you will need to be nominated by the union. You will be required to complete a short application form that will need to be signed by an authorised union official.

Progression routes

The progression routes depend on what type of learning you undertake. If you are a union representative or officer you will be able to improve your skills relevant to your post, which will enhance your chances of progression within the union. This may include courses in communication skills, organisational skills, health and safety, information technology and teamwork.

As an individual union member you can take part in education and learning programmes, and receive nationally recognised qualifications that can improve your promotion prospects or help you to apply for other jobs. Also, many adult learners decide to continue with their learning, undertaking courses at a level that they once thought they would be unable to achieve. They tend to find that the learning experience as an adult is much more positive than it had been at school, with supportive tutors and like-minded people on the course encouraging them to continue and succeed (see dialogue below).

The following piece of dialogue is from one of my focus group eval-uations of a group of adult learners taking part in a short course at an adult residential college, as part of their union learning. It illus-trates the personal benefits that can be gained from taking part in this type of course. *Catherine Dawson, 2009*

(Participant 1) When I first came here, I'm not a shy person but when I want to say things, when I open my mouth the wrong things come out. I was nervous speaking in groups, things like that, whereas now I've been about three or four times and I'm quite happy to speak in groups. You know, I've got more confidence through some of the courses I've been on.

(Participant 2) It's restored my confidence. I would certainly have not spoke in a group like this, no way. But because we did a course on confidence building it has helped me a lot.

(Participant 3) Well I've actually taken it one further, because of coming here I've became employed and I'm actually delivering one of our sessions for our group this week.

(Participant 2) We all come on the courses, there's about 11 of us and we've all spoke about it, confidence building, you know, the first time some of us came on the course, different courses, we sort of thought we were like nobodies, but now because of these courses that we've all done, we're somebody.

(Participant 4) Most of us came as nobodies and now we're somebodies.

Further information

Useful addresses

The Communication Workers Union can be contacted at:

CWU
150 The Broadway, Wimbledon, London SW19 1RX
Tel: (0208) 9717 200; Fax: (020) 8971 7300; e-mail: info@cwu.org;
website: www.cwu.org

The General Federation of Trade Unions can be contacted at:

GFTU Educational Trusts
Central House, Upper Woburn Place, London WC1H 0HY
Tel: (0207) 387 2578; Fax: (0207) 383 0820; e-mail: gftuhq@gftu.org.uk;
website: www.gftu.org.uk

The GMB can be contacted at:

GMB National Office
22/24 Worpole Road, London SW19 4DD
Tel: (020) 8947 3131; Fax: (020) 8944 6552; e-mail: info@gmb.org.uk;
website: www.gmb.org.uk

The National Union of Rail, Maritime and Transport Workers can be
contacted at:

RMT
Unity House, 39 Chalton Street, London NW1 1JD
Tel: (020) 7387 4771; Fax: (020) 7387 4123; e-mail: info@rmt.org.uk;
website: www.rmt.org.uk

The Union of Construction, Allied Trades and Technicians can be
contacted at:

UCATT General Office
177 Abbeville Road, London SW4 9RL
Tel: (0207) 622 2442; Fax: (0207) 720 4081; e-mail: info@ucatt.org.uk;
website: www.ucatt.info

Unison can be contacted at:

Unison Learning and Organizing Services
1 Mabledon Place, London WC1H 9AJ
Tel: (0845) 355 0845; Fax: (0207) 535 2105; e-mail: use contact form on
website: www.unison.org.uk

Unite can be contacted at:

Unite Education Department
Hayes Court, West Common Road, Hayes, Bromley, Kent BR2 7AU
Tel: (020) 8462 7755; Fax: (020) 8315 8234;
e-mail: education@unitetheunion.com;
website: www.unitetheunion.org.uk

Adult residential colleges

The six adult residential colleges are:

Coleg Harlech
Harlech, Gwynedd LL46 2PU
Tel: (01766) 781 900; Fax: (01766) 817 621; e-mail: use enquiry form on
website: www.harlech.ac.uk

Fircroft College
1018 Bristol Road, Selly Oak, Birmingham B29 6LH
Tel: (01214) 720 116; Fax: (01214) 725 481; e-mail: use contact form
on website: www.fircroft.ac.uk

Hillcroft College (for women)
South Bank, Surbiton, Surrey KT6 6DF
Tel: (020) 8399 2688; Fax: (020) 8390 9171; e-mail: use enquiry form on
website: www.hillcroft.ac.uk

Newbattle Abbey College
Dalkeith, Midlothian EH22 3LL
Tel: (0131) 663 1921; Fax: (0131) 654 0598;
e-mail: office@newbattleabbeycollege.ac.uk;
website: www.newbattleabbeycollege.ac.uk

Northern College
Wentworth Castle, Stainborough, Barnsley, South Yorkshire S75 3ET
Tel: (01226) 776 000; Fax: (01226) 776 025;
e-mail: courses@northern.ac.uk; website: www.northern.ac.uk

Ruskin College
Walton Street, Oxford OX1 2HE
Tel: (01865) 554 331; Fax: (01865) 554 372;
e-mail: enquiries@ruskin.ac.uk; website: www.ruskin.ac.uk

Useful websites

www.unionlearn.org.uk

This website has been established by the Trade Union Congress (TUC) to help unions to become learning organisations and spread the lifelong learning message. On this site you can access the unionlearn learning and careers advice service, which is a free, impartial and confidential service that helps people to develop new skills, improve their job prospects or change jobs. You can use the database to search more than 950,000 courses or obtain free expert advice by calling 08000 92 91 90.

www.skills4schools.org.uk

This website has been set up by UNISON to offer advice and guidance for school support staff. It provides information about personal development and career pathways, helping you to decide which course might be right for you and providing information about overcoming common barriers to learning.

Further reading

Information about the adult education bursary and other types of funding for adults who wish to study at university can be found in Dawson, C E (2009) *The Essential Guide to Paying for University: Effective funding strategies for parents and students*, London: Kogan Page (£9.99).

8 Learning through Work Scheme

The Learning through Work scheme is run by Learndirect and a number of partner universities and colleges. (Learndirect is an e-teaching organisation that was set up in 1998 as part of the University for Industry in England, Wales and Northern Ireland. It provides online courses, advice and guidance for learners and businesses.) If you are thinking of obtaining a university-level qualification, perhaps because you never had the chance to get a degree following the traditional route, or you would like to gain a postgraduate qualification directly related to your job, this scheme may be of interest to you. It enables you to study without leaving your job and is of benefit to the organisation for which you work. It also helps you to progress in your personal career.

This chapter describes the Learning through Work scheme and provides information about the level of wages, the eligibility criteria, application procedures and progression routes, concluding with useful websites and further reading.

Type of scheme

Through this scheme you can study a university-level course (at undergraduate or postgraduate level) without taking time off work. Learning involves projects you complete as part of your current working role, and tutor support is provided interactively online and face-to-face. This means that all your learning takes place in the workplace and that you do not need to attend a university or college to learn. You also receive your normal wage while you are working and learning.

Qualifications

You can choose to take different modules, all of which have a credit rating and these credits are added together to form your university qualification, which could be a degree or postgraduate qualification (for information about the different credit ratings and the qualifications to which they lead, visit the Learning through Work website, details below). You can choose how many modules you wish to take and can, therefore, build up your credit slowly at a time that suits you. You can also choose to take a number of short courses in subjects that are of interest to you and that will help you in your work. You can learn at any time throughout the year and at a pace that suits you.

It is possible to receive credits for your previous qualifications and for previous work experience, all of which will count towards your university qualification. This previous learning will be assessed by your tutor and approved through the quality assurance procedures of your university or college. You should note, however, that some colleges and universities may charge a fee to assess this previous learning.

The qualifications that you could work towards include:

- Certificate of Higher Education;
- Diploma of Higher Education/Foundation Degree;
- Honours Degree;
- Postgraduate Certificate;
- Postgraduate Diploma;
- Master's Degree.

Subject areas

Your learning plan is structured to meet your needs, which means that your personal Learning through Work programme may not, necessarily, fit into a traditional discipline or subject area. It is possible for you to pick and mix modules that suit your interests and the work that you undertake. Also, because most of your tutor interaction and assessment takes place online, you do not have to choose a college or university that is close to your place of work. Instead, you can choose a learning provider that offers the courses in which you are interested. The following list provides an example of the type of subject areas that you could choose:

- marketing;
- education;
- nursing studies and midwifery;
- finance;
- information technology;
- engineering;
- logistics;
- business;
- library and information studies;
- legal advice (housing, employment, debt);
- public services management;
- health and social care.

College and universities

At the time of writing the following colleges and universities are taking part in the Learning through Work programme:

- University of Chester;
- University of Derby;
- Northumbria University;
- University of Northampton;
- Staffordshire University;
- Wakefield College;
- University of the West of England, Bristol;
- Trinity College (Carmarthen).

Visit the Learning through Work website for information about the courses offered by each of these colleges and universities, and to obtain contact details of the person dealing with the scheme at each institution (details below).

Assessment procedures

Although you will not be required to take examinations, you will be required to produce some of the following so that they can be assessed by your tutor:

- business plans;
- portfolios of evidence;
- essays/assignments;
- software programmes, websites or critiques;
- personal research;
- management reports;
- creative projects;
- dissertation (a detailed report of the personal research that you have undertaken).

Amount of money

You will be paid your usual salary while you are learning. However, there is a cost for each module so you will need to find out how much this is before you enrol. In some cases your employer may agree to pay for the module (especially if it will help the business to grow), and/or they may help you by offering paid time off for learning.

Recently, the Learning through Work programme has teamed up with the Helena Kennedy Foundation (HKF) to offer learners a £500 bursary to help with their studies. You will also have the opportunity to take part in the mentoring and skills development programmes run by the Foundation. You will need to meet the eligibility criteria set out by the Foundation to apply for a bursary. For more information about this scheme and to find out whether you qualify, contact the HKF (details below).

Once you enrol on a course you become a student at the relevant college or university. This means that you can take advantage of the financial discounts that are available to all students, such as those offered on books, materials and stationery at students' union shops, and all the discounts and special offers available through the National Union of Students (NUS) (see the case study below). As a full- or part-time student over the age of 16 you can purchase an NUS Extra card, which is a student discount card that can be bought from the NUS for £10 (2009 prices). It enables you to obtain further discounts on books, entertainment, food, drinks and clothes. To find out more about these discount schemes, visit the NUS website (details below).

I am studying for a Certificate of Higher Education in Professional Work-based Studies at Trinity College. It's great and I'm loving it. I've just finished a module on research methods and that was great as I can really relate it to what I'm doing in work, well, I've just completed some research which is all part of the course and I should get credits for it and it's been something I had to do at work anyway... Apart from the study being really interesting, what I've found so useful is all the benefits I can get as a student... Well, I thought I would be too old, you know, in my 30s, but there's loads of us oldies there, and I can go and use the facilities and all that... I was surprised I could do that because I'm working and everything, you know, get cheap books and that. There's a shop and a union bar for the evenings if I'm at the library. *Kathryn, Kidwelly, Carmarthenshire*

Eligibility criteria

To qualify for the Learning through Work scheme you must be employed or self-employed and working at an appropriate level. The scheme is open to workers in any part of the United Kingdom, and is even available for workers who undertake some of their work overseas. Although you do not need any formal qualifications to take part in this scheme, you will have to satisfy the university or college that you are able to cope with the level of learning required on the programme. The Learning through Work programme has been designed to make higher education as accessible as possible, so previous work experience, and previous qualifications if you have any, will be taken into account when your eligibility is assessed.

Learning through Work will not enable you to obtain a degree that leads to a licence to practise qualification, such as a qualified nurse or teacher. However, if you are already a qualified professional you can take part in this scheme as part of your continuing professional development.

Application procedure

Before you apply for the scheme it would be useful to discuss your plans with your employer as they might have some useful advice to offer or may be able to help you to plan your learning around your job.

Applications for the scheme are made through the Learning through Work website (details below). To start the application process you will need to register with the service, supplying a username and password. Once you have completed the application form it will be sent to the college or university that you have selected, which will review your form and get back to you in due course (the length of time depends on the college or university). Some may request more information from you before they can say whether your application has been successful. If your application has not been successful they will explain why this is the case.

Progression routes

The Learning through Work programme provides the opportunity for you to receive formal credit for work and qualifications that you have already undertaken, and enables you to build up more credits for workplace learning. You will be able to use your learning for your own personal benefit and for the benefit of your employer (or for your company or business, if you are self-employed). You could be offered promotion or a higher salary to recognise the learning you have undertaken, or your own business could grow and flourish as a result of your learning.

Higher-level qualifications will also enable you to seek out more specialised working opportunities that may attract higher wages and greater job satisfaction, or you may decide to set up your own business and/or continue your learning at a higher level.

Further information

Useful websites

www.learningthroughwork.org
This website provides all the information you need about the Learning through Work scheme, including how the scheme works, eligibility criteria and available subject areas. You can make an online application through this website and use the online contact form to request more information.

www.hkf.org.uk
This website provides information about the Helena Kennedy Foundation, including details of the bursaries and mentoring programme, and the eligibility criteria for students who wish to apply for a bursary. The Foundation supports disadvantaged students who have overcome significant barriers in order to continue with their education at university level.

www.nussl.co.uk
This is the website of NUS Services, which is owned by students' unions and the NUS. Its mission is to 'create, develop and sustain competitive advantages for member Students' Unions – reducing costs and maximising commercial revenues'. Through NUS Services students' unions can obtain goods and marketing services at reduced prices and savings can be passed onto students.

www.nus.org.uk
The NUS is a voluntary membership organisation that represents the interests of students across the United Kingdom. You can obtain a wide range of information about all aspects of university life from the NUS, including information about the discounts that you could receive as a student. You can purchase an NUS Extra card from this site.

Further reading

Information about all aspects of paying for university, including discounts, grants and bursaries that are available for students, can be found in Dawson, C E (2009) *The Essential Guide to Paying for University: Effective funding strategies for parents and students*, London: Kogan Page (£9.99).

9 Investors in People

The Investors in People standard was developed in the early 1990s by a partnership of leading businesses and national organisations to help employers improve performance and realise their objectives through the management and development of their people. It is a voluntary scheme that aims to improve organisational performance through better planning, implementation and evaluation of learning and development programmes. If your employer has Investors in People status, it has made a commitment to its employees to help to improve their skills, knowledge and motivation.

This chapter describes the Investors in People scheme and provides information about the level of wages, the eligibility criteria, application procedures and progression routes, concluding with useful websites.

Type of scheme

For an organisation to succeed it is recognised that employees have the right knowledge, skills and motivation to work efficiently and effectively. However, it is acknowledged that all organisations are different so Investors in People provides a flexible framework that any organisation can adapt for its own requirements. The scheme is based on three principles:

1. *Plan:* developing strategies to improve the performance of the organisation. This could include developing education and training courses for employees.
2. *Do:* taking action to improve the performance of the organisation. This could include the delivery of training and/or enabling employers to take time off for extra study/training.
3. *Review:* evaluating the impact on the performance of the organisation. Employees who have completed their training will be given extra

responsibilities, and employers should carry out a periodic review to evaluate the impact of education and training schemes.

If your employer has achieved Investors in People status, or if it is interested in working towards this achievement, it should be willing to help its workforce to develop. Therefore, if your employer has not already approached you with suggestions, you should arrange a meeting to discuss your personal development needs, illustrating how this can help the performance of the organisation. Suitable education and training can then be arranged, either in-house or with an external learning provider.

As part of its commitment to Investors in People, your employer may also decide to arrange career development/information opportunities such as work shadowing, work experiences and job rotation. Alternatively, it may provide workshops on personal development topics, team building away-days or social events, all of which should help to improve the performance and motivation of employees (see quotation below).

Information for employers

If you are an employer, or if your employer does not have Investors in People status, you may be interested in finding out more about what it entails. If so, the Investors in People website has all the information you will require (including contact details of your local Investors in People Centre) to help you, or your employer, to begin to work towards this standard (details below). You can use the 'self-check' facility on the Investors in People website, which enables you to find out how you stand, currently, against the Investors in People Framework. Once you have answered 32 questions the tool has a simple traffic light report that outlines where you have met the requirements of the Framework or where you, or your employer, would need to undertake further development work.

There are other useful tools on this website for employers. These include a 'health and well-being at work tool', which helps you to review how your organisation currently supports the health and well-being of employees, and a 'business issue scoping tool', which enables you to identify the business issues relevant to your organisation and find out which areas of the Investors in People Framework can help you to develop.

I have a small business employing eight members of staff. We have been in existence for nearly 10 years. When I first set up the business I tried to do everything myself. It was pointed out to me that this was because I had a problem trusting other members of staff to work to the standard I required. I thought clients would only want to speak to the boss, rather than junior members of staff. For a while motivation was low and staff turnover was high. I had too much work on to have to think about recruitment all the time. So I decided to look into Investors in People. One of my good friends had just finished a Master's Degree at Lancaster University and he had conducted his research on this issue. He felt it could help me to improve the situation in my firm, but he also pointed out I had to trust my staff to do their work properly. In fact he also carried out rather an informal needs assessment for us.

I spoke to somebody about the Investors in People initiative and received a good deal of advice tailor-made to my firm. Our closest centre was in Abingdon, so that made it convenient and easy. I have not got time to go into all the detail, but through working with the centre and helping my staff to develop within our firm, I have reduced staff turnover significantly and I must say that members of staff appear to be much happier. I am open to suggestions from them, and all of them have developed their skills, with one of them even completing a university degree. That is excellent for her and for us. I have more time to spend at home and I have no problem delegating now. My staff are very well trained, and the situation is ongoing. We also socialise with each other now at least once a month, which never happened before. *Michael, owner of a small business based near Oxford, via e-mail*

Amount of money

You will receive your usual wage while you are learning. If your employer is committed to Investors in People, it will provide paid time off for study and some may even provide small grants or expenses to help you to take part in education and training. Speak to your employer to find out what is available.

Eligibility criteria

There are no set eligibility criteria for this scheme. All you need to do is speak to your employer to find out whether the organisation for which you work has Investors in People status. If so, you will know that your employer is committed to the development of its workforce and it should be open to any suggestions that you might have about how you can improve your education and training for the benefit of the organisation. The scheme is available in all parts of the United Kingdom and the standard has been licensed to a number of other countries.

Application procedure

In the first instance you should speak to your employer to find out whether it has achieved Investors in People status, and if it has not, whether it would be interested in doing so (some employers will arrange an internal awareness campaign to show employees that they have Investors in People status). You can then discuss your training requirements. The application procedure will depend on the type of course that you wish to undertake. If the training is conducted in-house you may only require your supervisor to put your name forward. If the course is with an external provider, in most cases you will need to apply direct to that learning provider, perhaps with a reference from your employer.

Progression routes

Research by the Institute of Employment Studies (IES) has found that an organisation achieving the Investors in People standard gains, on average, an extra £176 per employee in gross profit, every year. This illustrates that, should your employer decide to work towards this standard, profits should increase. However, this is not the only benefit. As an employee you may be given more responsibility at work, which could increase your motivation and personal job satisfaction. It will also improve your skills, confidence and transferable skills if you should decide to apply for promotion or another job at a later date.

Further information

Useful websites

www.investorsinpeople.co.uk
This website contains all the information an employer needs about Investors in People. Your employer can click on the map to find the contact details of the nearest Investors in People Centre. Here staff will be able to offer advice about how a company can achieve Investors in People status and illustrate the benefits that can be gained from working towards the standard.

www.investorsinpeoplechampions.co.uk
This is the website of the Champions Programme, which is about recognising and rewarding organisations and encouraging them to disseminate and share their best practices to other organisations of all sizes and within every sector. The examples on the website provide useful and interesting information for any employer interested in the Investors in People scheme.

10 Train to Gain

Train to Gain is a government national skills service that supports employers of all sizes in all sectors by offering advice on improving business performance through training. It also helps businesses to find funding for training employees. If you are employed, self-employed, a volunteer or an agency worker, and you want to improve your knowledge and skills through undertaking work-based learning, this scheme may provide the opportunity for you to do so. The Train to Gain scheme is only available in England. However, there are similar schemes available in other parts of the United Kingdom and more information about these schemes can be obtained from the websites listed below.

This chapter describes the Train to Gain scheme in England and provides information about the amount of funding, the eligibility criteria, application procedures and progression routes, concluding with useful websites and contact numbers.

Type of scheme

Through this scheme businesses are put in touch with a skills broker, college or training provider. These people work with the business to undertake the following tasks:

- identify training needs;
- create a tailored package of training;
- find reliable local trainers (to conduct in-house or external training);
- find funding to help businesses pay for the training;
- evaluate the training.

There are a variety of courses and qualifications that you, as an employee, can undertake as part of this scheme, including:

- National Vocational Qualifications (see Chapter 21);
- Apprenticeships (see Chapters 1, 2, 3 and 4);
- leadership and management training;
- bespoke courses, tailored to the needs of you and your employment;
- basic skills (literacy, numeracy and English language);
- sector-specific skills.

Train to Gain works with the Sector Skills Councils (SSCs) to identify the specific skills needs of each business sector and each skills broker will have the expertise to offer sector-specific skills advice. As an employee this scheme will help you to access specialist training relevant to your work. (SSCs are state-sponsored organisations that have been set up to help improve business productivity, reduce skills gaps and shortages and improve the supply of learning and training to enhance the skills of the workforce. Currently there are 25 SSCs that cover specific economic sectors in the United Kingdom.)

Ryland Roofing is based in Northamptonshire and now employs 15 members of staff. However, this was not always the case. Initially, John Ryland had been reluctant to take on permanent members of staff because he was worried that work contracts would dry up and that he would be paying people for 'hanging around'. However, the number of contracts taken on increased rapidly and John found that he was unable to call upon temporary workers at short notice, especially as many of them had obtained other short-term work. John began to recruit full-time workers and, having worked on a variety of building sites himself, knew the importance of making sure that members of staff were fully motivated and well-trained.

He initially found out about Train to Gain from 'an advert on telly'. He got in touch with a skills broker who was able to work with him to find suitable NVQ courses that would help his staff to gain the skills and qualifications they would require to become specialist roofers. He also received 'a small amount of money' to help cover wages while staff were training. Through taking part in this type of training, members of staff could expand their skills and take on additional work when required. John believes he has a 'good team' working for him, and that his company will go 'from strength to strength', even in the present economic climate. *Ryland Roofing, Northamptonshire*

Amount of money

You will continue to receive your usual wage while you are training (the scheme provides a contribution to wage costs for small businesses with less than 50 employees, which helps employers to cover the cost of training and enables them to continue paying employees their usual wage: see case study above). Some employers will provide paid time off for additional study and may help you with your expenses if you have to train at a distance from your home.

Eligibility criteria

To be eligible for the Train to Gain scheme you must be a full-time or part-time employee, self-employed, a volunteer or an employment agency worker, living and working in England. If you live and work elsewhere in the United Kingdom, visit the relevant website listed below to find out about similar schemes in your area. There are no age limits or qualification requirements for this scheme.

Application procedure

As the Train to Gain service helps employers to get the right training for their employees, it is your employer who must start the ball rolling. Speak to your employer about the possibilities available through this scheme. If employers want more information, they can visit the Train to Gain website or contact the skills broker helpline (details below). Alternatively, they can contact the local college or training provider, or seek further advice from the Business Link website or helpline (details below). It might help you to convince your employer of the benefits of the scheme if you point out that funds are available to help with training. For example, for organisations in the private sector with five to 250 employees, Train to Gain offers an in-depth skills analysis for owner/managers, plus grant support of up to £1,000 to develop leadership and management skills. More information about other types of funding is available on the Train to Gain website.

If your employer is interested in taking part in the scheme it will be put in touch with a skills broker, college or training provider who will be able to work with the employer to make sure that you get the type of training that you require. Speak to your employer about this so that you can make sure you are happy with what is arranged on your behalf. The training could be in-house, in which case you will not need to complete an application form. If external training is required you may need to complete a short application form provided by the college or training provider.

Progression routes

Research carried out by the Learning and Skills Council (LSC) suggests that, with the right skills, you could improve your earning potential by up to £3,000 a year. This could be through achieving promotion with your present employer, or you could choose to move to a more highly paid job with more responsibility. Improving your skills and knowledge through training could increase your motivation levels and improve job satisfaction, in addition to opening up new career directions.

Further information

Useful websites

www.traintogain.gov.uk

This website contains all the information you need to know about Train to Gain and contains a sub-category for employees. Your employer can be directed to this site so that it can find out how the scheme will benefit its business. It can find out how the scheme is organised and read about eligibility and possible sources of funding. There is a contact form available for employers who wish to contact a skills broker.

www.businesslink.gov.uk

Practical advice for businesses is available on this website, including information about finance and grants, employing people and growing a business. You can access a training directory with a link to work-related training courses on the Learndirect business website (www.learndirect. co.uk/businessinfo). You can also obtain contact details of your local Business Link service by using the postcode locator service on the site.

www.lds4b.com

This is the Learndirect Scotland for Business site, which provides details of support schemes available for businesses in Scotland. The site contains useful fact sheets about what is available, and a course search of over 18,000 courses and training workbooks to download. If you live in Scotland your employer can be directed to this site to find out more about help for its business, or it can ring the helpline for advice or to make an appointment with its local training provider: 08456 000 111.

http://wales.gov.uk

Visit this site and click on the 'education and skills' section, followed by the 'information for employers' section for information and advice for businesses in Wales. Guides are divided into three categories: information for businesses new to training; information for businesses needing to get better training; and information for larger organisations seeking skills excellence. More information about the schemes available can be obtained from 0845 60 661 60 or by e-mailing info@skillspeoplesuccess.com.

www.delni.gov.uk

Visit this site and click on the 'skills and training' section to access information about the training opportunities available for businesses in Northern Ireland. Your employer can find more information about Essential Skills training (reading, writing, maths and English) and Management Analysis and Planning (MAP), which enables an organisation, with the assistance of a business consultant, to complete an online assessment of its management and leadership development needs.

www10.employersguide.org.uk

This website provides an employer's guide to training. Your employer can access this service to search for a training provider in your area. It can search the database by keyword and postcode. The search results provide information about the type of course, duration, attendance and the qualifications that can be achieved.

http://inourhands.lsc.gov.uk
Visit the 'learners' section of this website to obtain more information about learning new skills and gaining qualifications. There are some interesting case studies and useful links to other relevant sites. Your employer can access the 'employers' section for more information about how improving the skills and training of its employees can help the business.

Useful telephone numbers

Your employer can contact a skills broker for more information and advice about Train to Gain: 0800 015 55 45.
Your employer can contact the Business Link Helpline for practical advice about all aspects of running a business: 0845 600 9006.
Contact Learndirect business for more information about work-related training courses: 0800 101 901.

Part Two

Learning and Earning in Further Education

11 Part-time Learning and Earning

The first part of this book has discussed the different learning and earning schemes that are available for people through their workplace. This part looks at the schemes that are available in the further education sector.

This chapter discusses the different learning opportunities that are available for people who want to continue their learning at further education level while they are earning a wage in full- or part-time employment. It goes on to discuss the amount of money that may be available for this type of learning, the eligibility criteria, application procedures and progression routes, concluding with useful websites and further reading.

Type of scheme

'Further education' refers to education undertaken after the compulsory school-leaving age (currently 16 in all parts of the United Kingdom, although there are plans to increase this to 18 by 2015). Qualifications at this level include A levels, BTECS and NVQs up to Level 3. There are various types of organisation offering courses at further education level, as described below.

FE colleges, tertiary colleges and community colleges

These colleges offer a wide range of courses to students of all ages. Courses can be during the day, during the evening, full-time, part-time, day release or block release. Qualifications can be academic or vocational. Visit the relevant website listed below to access contact details of your local college:

● If you live in Northern Ireland visit the Association of Northern Ireland Colleges website (www.getoncourse.org). This website provides a gateway to all six further education colleges in Northern Ireland.

- If you live in Scotland visit the Association of Scotland's Colleges website (www.ascol.org.uk). This website contains contact details of all of Scotland's FE colleges.
- If you live in England or Wales visit the Association of Colleges website (www.aoc.co.uk) for contact details of your local FE college.

Sixth form colleges

These colleges are designed for 16–18-year-olds and tend to be attached to schools. Courses usually run during normal school hours and qualifications can be academic or vocational. To find out which sixth form colleges are available in England, download the location map available on the Sixth Form Colleges' Forum website (www.sfcf.org.uk). Alternatively, students from England, Wales and Scotland can use the search facility at www.upmystreet.com to find contact details of your local sixth form college.

If you are interested in independent school sixth forms, enter your postcode in the school locator at www.independentschools.com. This service includes independent schools in all parts of the United Kingdom.

Specialist colleges

Throughout the United Kingdom there are a number of colleges that specialise in offering further education in specific subject areas such as art and design, music or childcare. Agricultural colleges are also included in this category. Although these colleges used to concentrate on purely agricultural areas such as farming and horticulture, they now offer related courses in areas such as business and estate management.

If you live at a distance from one of these colleges, and the specialist course is not available locally, you may be entitled to receive a residential bursary if you choose to study full-time at the college. To find a list of specialist colleges, including contact details, and for further information about bursaries and eligibility criteria, visit http://moneytolearn.direct.gov.uk/residentialbursary.

Adult residential colleges

These colleges specialise in offering both short- and long-term courses for adults in a supportive, residential environment. Most colleges define adults as over the age of 21 and some will not offer places on their long courses to anyone who has already achieved qualifications at higher education level. These colleges usually offer short courses, access courses (which enable entry to higher education on successful completion) and perhaps the first year of a degree course. There is a wide range of short course subjects on offer and these vary between colleges: some specialise in arts subjects, others in social and community issues, others in information technology.

To find an adult residential college visit the Adult Residential Colleges Association website (www.arca.uk.net) and click on the relevant college to be directed to its website.

Adult Education Service

Many local authorities run their own adult education service. These provide courses aimed specifically at adults. Some may lead to vocational qualifications, others to academic qualifications, or many courses are offered for interest, without leading to a specific qualification. Some adult education services run 'bite size' or 'taster courses' for adults who are unsure of what they would like to study. Look in the *Yellow Pages* under 'adult education' or 'further education', or contact your local Citizen's Advice Bureaux or local authority to find out about your local service. In many towns and cities a free prospectus is delivered to your home or made available in the local library.

The Workers' Educational Association (WEA)

This is a registered charity, founded in 1903. It aims to provide high quality learning opportunities for adults from all walks of life, but especially those who may have missed out on learning in early life, or who are socially and economically disadvantaged. The WEA is non-party-political and works closely with a range of partners including local authorities, universities and other voluntary and community organisations. Courses are organised by over 600 local branches throughout the United Kingdom. To find a WEA course near to you, use the postcode locator tool at www.wea.org.uk.

Distance learning, correspondence learning and online courses

These courses provide the opportunity to learn in your home at a pace that suits you. They are useful for people who have caring commitments or for those who are unable to leave the home for other reasons, such as mobility restrictions or work commitments. It is also a useful way of learning for those people who might be uncomfortable about entering an unfamiliar learning environment.

The Open University (OU) is perhaps one of the best known distance learning providers at higher education level (see Chapter 25). At further education level you may want to consider organisations such as the National Extension College (www.nec.ac.uk), the Open College (www.opencollege.info) or learndirect (www.learndirect.co.uk). You should note, however, that some of these courses can be very expensive, so you should make sure that you are very clear about costs before you enrol.

There are many other learning providers that offer distance learning courses, but you should check that they are accredited before enrolling by visiting the Open and Distance Learning Quality Council website (www.odlqc.org.uk). This site contains useful advice about choosing a course, knowing about costs and what to do if things go wrong. It also lists, and provides contact details of, all accredited distance learning providers.

Amount of money

If you choose to study part-time while you are working you will continue to receive your usual wage. Some employers may also help with your learning by agreeing to some paid time off for study.

If you want to study at further education level, there are various funds available for which you may qualify:

- *Education Maintenance Allowance (EMA):* this scheme pays a weekly payment and periodic bonuses to young people to encourage them to stay on at school or college (see Chapters 12, 13, 14 and 15).
- *Individual Learning Accounts (Wales and Scotland):* these schemes provide small grants to people who are claiming means-tested benefits (or earning less than £22,000 in Scotland), or who do not have

qualifications above Level 2 to help with their learning (see Chapters 16 and 17).

- *Adult Learning Grant (England):* this scheme provides a weekly grant to adults who take part in full-time study. The amount you will receive is income-assessed, so if you have a part-time job it could affect the amount of grant received (see Chapter 18).
- *City & Guild bursaries:* these may be available for students studying for a City & Guilds qualification (see Chapter 19).
- *Career development loans:* these provide a loan to help cover the cost of course fees, up to £8,000 (see Chapter 20).
- *Childcare support schemes:* if you have children there are various support schemes and funds available to help you to find, and pay for, childcare while you are studying (see Chapter 23).
- *Discretionary learner support funds:* throughout the United Kingdom there is a variety of extra funding schemes to help students who are facing financial hardship while they study. You may qualify for some of these schemes if you wish to study at further education level (see Chapter 24).

Eligibility criteria

Course eligibility

The eligibility criteria will depend on the course that you wish to undertake. Some will require previous qualifications, while others will not. Eligibility criteria for all courses should be clearly displayed in the prospectus/course information pack. If in doubt, speak to the course or admissions tutor.

Funding eligibility

Visit the relevant chapters of this book to find out whether you are eligible for funding for study at further education level. Some funding, such as the EMA, depends on your age, whereas other funding is based on criteria such as household income and whether or not you have children or other dependants.

Application procedure

Course applications

Although application and enrolment procedures may differ slightly from college to college, in general you will need to follow the procedure set out below:

> *Step 1:* obtain an up-to-date prospectus or consult the college website. These should contain information about how to enrol for a course.
>
> *Step 2:* if you cannot find the right course, the prospectus or website should contain an information number or an e-mail address that you can use to discuss your choices with a trained adviser.
>
> *Step 3:* complete the request form, either online or from the prospectus. This enables you to select a course, or courses, in which you are interested and request the relevant information. Course information and an enrolment form will be posted or e-mailed to you, or you could pick up the information in person from your local college.
>
> *Step 4:* read the course information carefully to check that it meets your requirements. If you have any doubts contact the college to speak to a trained adviser or to the course tutor. Make sure that you are completely clear about the costs involved.
>
> *Step 5:* fill in and return your enrolment form, by post, e-mail or by attending an enrolment day. Most colleges will enable students to speak to specialist staff on the day who will be able to discuss the options available, including tailor-made courses and flexible provision.
>
> *Step 6:* some colleges run an induction day designed to help you to become familiar with the college and facilities before you start your course. It is useful to attend the induction day as you will be shown useful services such as the library and computing facilities.

If you intend to apply for a distance learning or online course, you may not have the opportunity to discuss your requirements with an adviser, so you must read all course information carefully and make sure that you are clear about costs, regulations and requirements before completing the enrolment form. Visit www.odlqc.org.uk for comprehensive advice about choosing and applying for a distance learning course.

Funding applications

Read the relevant chapter of this book for information about how to apply for funding. Before applying you will need to make sure that you meet the eligibility criteria and that you have all the necessary information to hand, such as details of household income or proof of benefits claimed. Most applications for funding will require you to complete an application form and attach all the relevant supporting evidence.

Progression routes

Learning at further education level can lead to a wide variety of opportunities, within both education and employment. Many people find that their new skills and qualifications help them to apply for promotion in their existing job, or enable them to take on additional responsibilities that could lead to a higher salary. Others find that better qualifications and increased confidence and self-belief help them to apply for new jobs with more job satisfaction and higher salaries.

Some people find that they enjoy their learning and have succeeded well above their initial expectations (see the case study below). This enables them to think about continuing their learning at higher education level, either on a full- or part-time basis. If you are interested in continuing your learning at university, there is a variety of schemes available that help you to learn while you earn a wage. These are discussed in Part III of this book.

I were so scared when I first went, you know, I didn't know what to expect. I thought they'd all be like really young or something. But it weren't like that at all. They were all like me, you know, scared and stuff. But we knuckled down, like, and it were great... Well, now I want to carry on, you know, I've like got the bug, the learning bug, you know. I didn't know I could do it. It were such a surprise to me and even more to me husband. Such a surprise. So now I'm going to university. Me, can you believe it? Me mum would have been so shocked. *Jaine, 44, Sheffield*

Further information

Useful websites

http://moneytolearn.direct.gov.uk
More information about all aspects of funding for further education in England and Wales can be obtained from this site.

www.scotland.gov.uk/topics/education
More information about funding for study at further education level in Scotland can be obtained from this site.

www.delni.gov.uk/index/further-and-higher-education.htm
More information about funding for study at further education level in Northern Ireland can be obtained from this site.

http://careersadvice.direct.gov.uk
Visit this site for useful information about all aspects of jobs, careers and learning, including information about sources of funding that may be available to you. You can use the tools available on this site to assess your skills and interests and help you to produce a CV when you start to look for work.

https://skillsaccounts.direct.gov.uk
Skills accounts were piloted in England in 2009 and it is hoped that they will be available to everyone over the age of 19 throughout England in 2010. Skills accounts offer advice about sources of support to help you with your learning and provide course information, so that you can understand the options available to you when deciding about your skills and career. 'Skills vouchers' are being piloted as part of this scheme in the East Midlands and South East regions of England. These show what funding may be available for your chosen course. Visit this website for more information about the scheme and to register your details.

Further reading

For a comprehensive guide to further education consult the *Directory of Vocational and Further Education*, which you should be able to find in the reference section of your local library. It is a complete guide to FE courses in the United Kingdom and includes informative articles on further education and the qualifications that can be gained.

12 Education Maintenance Allowance (England)

The Education Maintenance Allowance (EMA) was introduced in September 2004 in England, Wales and Northern Ireland and in 2005 in Scotland. The schemes differ slightly in each of these parts of the United Kingdom so you will need to obtain the information relevant to the place in which you intend to study (see Chapters 13, 14 and 15). Through this scheme a weekly payment and periodic bonuses are paid to young people to encourage them to stay on at school or college. If you intend to study in England and you are aged 16–18 you may qualify for the EMA if you are from a low income household.

This chapter describes the EMA scheme in England and provides information about the amount of money, the eligibility criteria, application procedures and progression routes, concluding with useful websites and contact numbers.

Type of scheme

This scheme pays a means-tested weekly allowance to all qualifying students aged 16–18 who intend to carry on with their learning after their compulsory schooling. To receive this weekly allowance you must agree to sign, and adhere to, a 'learning agreement'. This needs to be signed by you, your parents and your school or college. However, if you are estranged from your parents and considered 'independent' you will not need a parental signature. The agreement includes issues such as attendance, behaviour and completing the required amount of homework. Your payments may discontinue if you are deemed to have broken the agreement.

In addition to this weekly payment, you may also receive additional bonuses if you have full attendance, do well on your course and meet the targets set by your teacher, tutor or training provider. Weekly payments and bonuses are not affected by any part-time wages you may receive and if your parents are on benefits their payment will not be affected by the EMA.

Amount of money

At the time of writing the figures for 2010/11 had not been set. As a general guide, the Government set the following funding levels for entry in the academic year 2009/10 (levels are based on your household income for the previous tax year):

- £30 per week where family income is below £20,817.
- £20 per week where family income is between £20,818 and £25,521.
- £10 per week where family income is between £25,522 and £30,810.
- Periodic bonus of £100 if the learning agreement is satisfied. These could be earned in January, July and October if you return for a second year. This gives the opportunity to earn an extra £500 on top of your weekly allowance, for a two-year course.

The money will be paid straight into your bank account so you will need to make sure that you have a bank account before you apply for the EMA. The money is intended to help with course-related costs such as travel, books and equipment. However, once the money is in your bank account it is up to you how you decide to spend the cash.

The EMA guarantee

The 'EMA guarantee' means you get EMA payments automatically at the same rate for up to three years, even if your household income goes up. This applies up to the year in which you reach the age of 19. This means that, if your circumstances have not changed, you will not need to complete a new application form and your payments will continue once your course resumes.

Eligibility criteria

You will qualify for payment if you meet the following conditions:

- Your household income is below £30,810 per year (2008/09 threshold).
- You meet the age requirements (aged 16–18).
- You must be intending to enrol on one of the following:
  - a full-time further education course at a college or school;
  - an LSC-funded Diploma (where available) or a course that leads to an Apprenticeship;
  - an LSC-funded Entry to Employment (e2e) course.
- You are a UK national, or have been granted indefinite leave to remain or refugee status, or you are from a European Union or European Economic Area country. If you are in doubt about your status, more information can be obtained from www.homeoffice.gov.uk.

I think it did help Mark, yes, I think it helped him to make his mind up about staying on at school. Some of his mates had got jobs and were earning, which appealed to him, but we wanted him to stay on and do his A Levels... Because Simon had been made redundant he could qualify for the payment... I know £30 a week doesn't sound a lot but it was enough to sway his decision. So me and Simon were very happy really... He's quite clever and it would have been a waste if he'd not gone on... I'd like him to go to university but we'll cross that bridge when it comes. *Alison, 49, Weymouth*

Application procedure

You can request an application pack by telephone (0800 121 8989). Alternatively, you can obtain an EMA application pack from your school, college, training provider or local Connexions service. You can apply for an EMA at any time during the year. However, if you wish your payments to be backdated to the start of your course there is a deadline by which time your form must be returned. In general, it is advisable to apply as early as possible so that your payments are in place for the start of your course. You will need to complete the form and your parents or carer will need to provide evidence of their household income for the relevant tax year. This can be their Tax Credit Award Notice (TC602) or P60. You will also need to open a bank account and provide evidence, such as a bank statement or payment book.

Once you have completed your form and returned it with all the supporting evidence, your application will be assessed. If you qualify for the EMA a Notice of Entitlement (NOE) will be sent to you confirming the weekly amount you will receive. You will need to keep this form and take it with you when you enrol on your course. Your school, college or learning provider will then ask you to sign your learning agreement, mentioned above. Continued payment of the EMA is dependent on you not breaching this agreement.

Progression routes

Your progression route depends on the type of course you are undertaking, whether you enjoy your learning and wish to continue, or whether you wish to obtain a job at the end of your course. If you are studying for A levels or a diploma, you may wish to continue your learning by applying for university. If this is the case, and you are from a low income household, there are a variety of grants available to help you to pay for your university education. More information about the different types of learning and earning schemes that are available for study at higher education level is provided in Part III of this book.

Alternatively, you may prefer to apply for a job once you have completed your learning, and if you have completed your course successfully you may find that there are more, and better paid, employment options open to you.

Further information

Useful websites

http://ema.direct.gov.uk
This is the Government EMA website. Here you can find more information about the EMA, including information about the eligibility criteria

and application process. This site also links to the Government information website (www.direct.gov.uk) which contains more information
about EMAs.

www.connexions-direct.com

This is the Connexions website, which provides information and advice
for young people. More information about EMAs can be obtained from
this site. You can also contact a Connexions Direct Adviser by phone on
080 800 132 19, by text on 07766 413 219, by textphone 08000 968 336,
or by e-mail (use the contact form available on the website).

Useful telephone numbers

You can get more advice about the EMA by ringing the Learner Support
helpline on 0800 121 8989.

13 Education Maintenance Allowance (Scotland)

EMAs were launched across Scotland in August 2005 to provide financial support to young people from low income families who wish to continue with their learning after compulsory schooling. The programme is managed by your local authority or your college. If you are from a low income family and you are aged 16–19 and intend to study in Scotland, this scheme could be of benefit to you.

This chapter describes the EMA scheme in Scotland and provides information about the amount of money, the eligibility criteria, application procedures and progression routes, concluding with useful websites.

Type of scheme

In Scotland the EMA is a weekly allowance that is paid to all qualifying students who have 100 per cent attendance on their course. It will be paid for all full weeks within term time, up to a maximum of 42 weeks in any one academic year. EMA payments are not made during short term-time holidays, which include the October week, Christmas and Easter. Extra bonuses are paid if you progress well on your course. You are eligible to receive EMA payments during your study/examination period as set out by the Scottish Qualifications Authority (SQA), provided you attend for all the examinations that are listed in your learning agreement. More information about the SQA can be obtained from www.sqa.org.uk.

If you are intending to study at college you can be on either an EMA or a maintenance bursary but not both. A maintenance bursary is an income-assessed bursary that is available for those studying full-time courses below HNC or SVQ Level 4 in Scotland. The amount of bursary can be up to £86.81 a week for self-supporting students (2009 figures), so you should speak to your college bursary officer to find out whether you are eligible to receive a bursary as it could be more than the EMA, which currently is a maximum of £30 a week. However, if you are in receipt of an EMA you may still be entitled to other forms of bursary support, for example a travel bursary. More information about the different types of bursary that may be available for college students in Scotland can be obtained from www.saas.gov.uk.

Amount of money

At the time of writing the 2010/11 income thresholds had not been announced. In 2009 students were paid the following amounts, according to household income:

Household income	Weekly payment
£0 – £21,835	£30
£21,836 – £26,769	£20
£26,770 – £32,316	£10
more than £32,317	£0

You may also be able to receive two periodic bonuses of £150 if you remain on your course and make good progress with your learning. Bonuses are paid out in January/February and June/July.

Eligibility criteria

To be eligible for the scheme you must meet the following conditions:

● You must be aged 16–19 (if you reach your 20th birthday while receiving an EMA, payments will stop from the week after your 20th birthday).
● You must have reached school leaving age.
● Your annual family income must be less than £32,317.
● You must be on a recognised full-time course of study, in a school or at college. Within the school sector, for EMA purposes 'full-time' means at least 21 guided learning hours per week.

- You must agree to, and sign, a learning agreement that sets out your responsibilities and what is expected of you. This must also be signed by your parents, unless you are estranged from them. A sample learning agreement can be downloaded from the EMA Scotland website (details below). A new learning agreement will need to be completed for each academic year.

Young people on the New Deal education option or on government-supported training schemes are not eligible for EMAs (see Chapter 37 for more information on New Deal).

Application procedure

Application forms can be obtained from your school, college or local authority (contact details for all colleges and local authorities in Scotland can be obtained from the EMA Scotland website: details below). A sample form can be viewed on this site, but cannot be downloaded.

You should apply as soon as you can so that your payments will not be delayed at the start of your course. It is possible to apply once your course has started and a certain number of payments will be backdated. However, there is a deadline for backdated payments, which is usually around six months after the start of your course, so you should make sure that you do not lose out on payments by missing the deadline. As payments are made directly to your bank, you will need to have opened a bank account prior to applying for the EMA.

Progression routes

Your progression route depends on the type of course you are undertaking, whether you enjoy your learning and wish to continue, or whether you wish to obtain a job at the end of your course. If you are studying at SVQ Level 3 or for your Highers, you may wish to continue your learning by applying for a university course. If this is the case most Scottish students who choose to study at university in Scotland do not have to pay tuition fees and there are other grants and bursaries available for your studies. There is also a variety of learning and earning schemes available for students who wish to study at higher education level and these are discussed in detail in Part III of this book.

Alternatively, you may prefer to apply for a job once you have completed your learning, and if you have completed your course successfully you may find that there are more, and better paid, employment options open to you. Careers Scotland provides comprehensive information about career choices, including education options, funding opportunities and making effective job applications (details below).

Further information

Useful websites

www.emascotland.com
This is the EMA Scotland website, which provides all the information you need to know about the EMA in Scotland. There is a section for administrators, current students and new students. You can download a sample learning agreement from this site and access contact details of colleges and local councils in Scotland.

www.careers-scotland.org.uk
This is the website of Careers Scotland where you can access comprehensive information about education and employment, including funding opportunities, choosing a career, producing a CV and attending interviews. If you would like some face-to-face advice you can use the postcode search facility to find your nearest careers centre.

14 Education Maintenance Allowance (Wales)

The EMA in Wales is a scheme that has been set up to encourage young people to stay on in full-time education, through providing an allowance to help them with the cost of their studies. The amount that you can receive depends on your household income. If you are aged 16–18 and you intend to study full-time on a course at school or college in Wales, this scheme may be of interest to you.

This chapter describes the EMA scheme in Wales and provides information about the amount of money, the eligibility criteria, application procedures and progression routes, concluding with useful websites and contact numbers.

Type of scheme

In Wales the EMA scheme pays a fortnightly allowance to all qualifying students to study on courses such as GCSEs, A levels, BTECs, NVQs or basic skills. There are also bonus payments for students who progress satisfactorily on their course. The money is intended to help to cover day-to-day course-related costs such as travel, books and equipment and is paid direct into your bank account. If you qualify for an EMA you will have to adhere to a learning agreement that covers issues such as attendance, performance and behaviour.

Amount of money

Students who started their course in the academic year 2009/10 received the following amounts, according to their household income (these income thresholds may be raised slightly for students starting their course in 2010/11):

Household income	Fortnightly EMA payment
Up to £21,885	£60
£21,886 – £26,840	£40
£26,841 – £32,400	£20
£32,400 and above	£0

Payments of the allowance will be made on a fortnightly basis direct into your bank account, so you must make sure that you have opened a bank account that can receive direct credits prior to applying for an EMA. Bonus payments of £100 may be available for students who progress well on their course and meet all the conditions set out in their learning agreement. These are usually paid in January and July.

An EMA calculator is available on the Student Finance Wales website to help you to work out how much money you could receive (details below).

Eligibility criteria

To be eligible for an EMA in Wales you must meet the following conditions:

- You must be aged 16–18 (for example, students who were studying in the academic year 2009/2010 must have had a date of birth on or between 1 September 1990 and 31 August 1993).
- You must be studying on an eligible course. Your school or college will be able to offer advice about this, but as a general guide the course should be:
  - an academic or vocational course up to and including Level 3;
  - full-time at school or a minimum of 12 guided hours a week at college;
  - at least 10 weeks in duration.

- You must agree to, and sign, a learning agreement that covers all attendance and performance rules set by your school or college. You must meet these in order to receive your weekly allowance and periodic bonuses.
- You must meet the residency requirements (these are set out in detail on the guidance notes that accompany the EMA application form).

Application procedure

Application forms and guidance notes can be downloaded from the Student Finance Wales website (details below). Online demonstrations are available to help you to complete the form. You should apply as soon as the application forms become available, which is usually in the spring prior to the start of the autumn academic year. If your form is not received within eight weeks of starting your course you may lose out on backdated EMA payments.

Once your application form has been assessed, you will receive a letter confirming whether you are eligible to receive the EMA. If you are, you will need to sign your learning agreement once you enrol on your course.

Progression routes

Your progression route depends on the type of course you are undertaking, whether you enjoy your learning and wish to continue, or whether you wish to obtain a job at the end of your course. If you are studying for A levels, a diploma or NVQ Level 3, you may wish to continue your learning by applying for university. If this is the case, and you are from a low income household, there are various bursaries and grants that are available to help you to finance your studies. These include an Assembly Learning Grant, Special Support Grant, university bursaries, travel grants and various grants for children and adult dependants. There is also a variety of learning and earning schemes available for people who want to study at higher education level while earning a wage; these are discussed in Part III of this book.

Alternatively, you may prefer to apply for a job once you have finished your studies, and if you have completed your course successfully you may find that there are more, and better paid, employment options open to you. It is also possible to continue your learning while working for an employer through the Apprenticeship scheme (see Chapter 3). More information about searching for jobs, finding an Apprenticeship and making applications is provided on the Careers Wales website (details below).

Further information

Useful websites

www.studentfinancewales.co.uk
This is the website of Student Finance Wales. Go to the EMA/ALG micro site to find more information about the EMA in Wales. (The ALG is an Assembly Learning Grant of up to £1,500, paid to students from low income families who are aged 19 or over, whereas the EMA is a fortnightly allowance paid to students aged 16–18 from low income households.) You can e-mail the EMA Wales Customer Services Team at EMAWALES@slc.co.uk for more information.

www.careerswales.com
Careers Wales is funded by the Welsh Assembly Government and gives free careers information, advice and guidance to people of all ages in Wales. Comprehensive information is available on all aspects of education and employment in Wales, including a CV wizard and interactive interview games. The service is available in English and Welsh.

Useful telephone numbers

You can phone the EMA Wales Customer Services Team on 0845 602 8845, Monday to Friday, 8:00 am to 8:00 pm and Saturday, 9:00 am to 1:00 pm.

15 Education Maintenance Allowance (Northern Ireland)

In Northern Ireland the EMA aims to encourage young people to stay on at school through providing a weekly allowance and periodic bonuses. If you are age 16–19, from a low income household and you intend to study full-time at school or college in Northern Ireland, this scheme may be of interest to you.

This chapter describes the EMA scheme in Northern Ireland and provides information about the amount of money, the eligibility criteria, application procedures and progression routes, concluding with useful websites and contact numbers.

Type of scheme

This scheme pays a weekly allowance and periodic bonuses to young people studying on courses at further education level in Northern Ireland (up to and including Level 3). This includes academic and vocational courses that lead to qualifications such as AS/A2, NVQs, GCSEs and Basic Skills Level 1.

The EMA is not available for courses at higher education level or for courses that attract a training allowance or grant, such as an FE Award. These are means-tested discretionary grants for students studying at further education level. You may find that you receive more money if you are awarded an FE Award (£2,050 per year in 2009/10), rather than an EMA, but funds are limited and discretionary, so you will need to find out whether you meet the eligibility criteria and whether funds are available before making your decision. For more information about FE Awards contact your local Education and Library Board (ELB) or visit the Department for Employment and Learning in Northern Ireland (DELNI) website (details below).

Amount of money

EMA entitlement is based on an assessment of your household income in the previous financial year. In 2009 students received the following amount, depending on their household income (income thresholds may rise slightly in 2010/11):

Household income	Weekly EMA
up to £21,885	£30
£21,886 – £26,840	£20
£26,841 – £32,400	£10
£32,401 or above	no award

There are also bonus payments of £100 if you remain on your course and make satisfactory progress with your learning. Payments are made direct to your bank so you will need to make sure that you have opened a bank account prior to applying for the EMA.

The EMA is intended to help with a variety of costs such as books, equipment, transport, contributing to family income and other costs incurred during a course of study. It is paid in addition to other financial support provided by the government such as the Working Family Tax Credit, Child Benefit and the Child Tax Credit. It will not be affected by any money that you might earn from a part-time job.

Eligibility criteria

To receive an EMA in Northern Ireland you will need to meet the following eligibility criteria:

- You must be aged 16, 17, 18 or 19 years.
- Your household income must be £32,400 or less.
- You must be undertaking at least 15 hours of guided learning at an FE college or studying full-time at school in Northern Ireland.

- You must meet the residency criteria (detailed information about these residency requirements is provided in the guidance notes that accompany the EMA application form).

Application procedure

You should apply for an EMA as soon as forms become available, before the start of the academic year (forms are usually available from April prior to the start of the autumn term). Forms can be obtained from your school, college, Job Centre or can be downloaded from the DELNI website (details below). Alternatively, you can telephone the EMA helpline (details below). Completed application forms should be sent to EMA Customer Services, Admail 3864, Belfast BT1 3ZY.

If your application is successful you will receive a Notice of Entitlement that explains how much you will receive. Once you have enrolled on your course you will be required to sign two parts of an EMA Contract. The first part covers what sessions you must attend and will include a Code of Behaviour from the learning provider; the second covers the specific learning goals that you must achieve to receive your periodic bonuses.

Progression routes

Your progression route depends on the type of course you are undertaking, whether you enjoy your learning and wish to continue, or whether you wish to obtain a job at the end of your course. If you are studying for A levels, a diploma or NVQ Level 3, you may wish to continue your learning by applying for a university place. If this is the case, and you are from a low income household, there are a variety of grants and bursaries available to help you to fund your studies. These include maintenance grants, Special Support Grants, university bursaries and various grants for childcare and adult dependants. Alternatively, you may be interested in learning while earning a wage. If this is the case there are various opportunities available and these are discussed in detail in Part III of this book.

If you prefer to apply for a job once you have completed your learning, and if you have completed your course successfully, you may find that there are wider choices available to you, because you have stayed on at school or college and have obtained more and higher level qualifications. If you are interested in applying for a job, you will find the Careers Service Northern Ireland website useful (details below).

Further information

Useful websites

www.delni.gov.uk
This is the website of the Department for Employment and Learning in Northern Ireland. Type 'EMA' into the search box to be directed to all the information you require about the EMA in Northern Ireland. Application forms and guidance notes can be downloaded from this site. You can also access useful information about other sources of funding for study in Northern Ireland.

www.careersserviceni.com
The Careers Service Northern Ireland has been developed to offer advice and guidance on learning, training and employment opportunities in Northern Ireland. The website contains contact details of careers services throughout Northern Ireland, along with comprehensive advice about writing a CV and covering letter. There are also useful tips about filling in application forms and attending a job interview.

www.belb.org.uk
This is the website of the Belfast Education and Library Board. If you live in Belfast visit this website for more information about education, training and funding in your area.

www.neelb.org.uk
This is the website of the North Eastern Education and Library Board. If you live in Antrim, Ballymena, Ballymoney, Carrickfergus, Coleraine, Larne, Magherafelt, Moyle or Newtownabbey, visit this website for more information about education, training and funding in your area.

www.seelb.org.uk
This is the website of the South Eastern Education and Library Board. If you live in Ards, Castlereagh, Down, Lisburn or North Down, visit this website for more information about education, training and funding in your area.

www.selb.org
This is the website of the Southern Education and Library Board. If you live in Armagh, Banbridge, Cookstown, Craigavon, Dungannon or Newry and Mourne, visit this website for more information about education, training and funding in your area.

www.welbni.org
This is the website of the Western Education and Library Board. If you live in Fermanagh, Limavady, Londonderry, Omagh or Strabane, visit this website for more information about education, training and funding in your area.

Useful telephone numbers

You can contact the EMA Customer Services Team for more information about the EMA on 0845 601 7646.

16 Individual Learning Accounts (Wales)

Individual Learning Accounts are available for people who live in Wales to help with the cost of learning on part-time courses. If you are aged 18 or over and you or your partner are claiming income-related benefits or you do not have any qualifications above Level 2, this scheme might be of interest to you.

This chapter describes the Individual Learning Account (ILA) scheme in Wales and provides information about the amount of money, the eligibility criteria, application procedures and progression routes, concluding with useful websites and contact numbers.

Type of scheme

ILA Wales has been set up for people on income-related benefits, or for those with little or no formal qualifications. The scheme pays a small grant to people living in Wales to help with the cost of learning. The money can be used to help to pay for a wide variety of part-time courses, which could be evening classes, day courses or distance learning courses. They may take place at colleges, universities or with other training providers. You can use the 'Learning Choices' section on the Careers Wales website to find a course suitable for your needs or you can telephone Learning and Careers Advice (details below) for further information.

Amount of money

This scheme will pay a grant to cover course costs, up to £200 for people who are claiming income-related benefits, and up to £100 for people who do not have any previous qualifications above Level 2 (see below for information about the different types of qualifications that qualify for funding).

Eligibility criteria

To be eligible for this scheme you must be 18 or over and living in Wales. If you or your partner are claiming any of the following income-related benefits, you will be able to receive a grant towards 100 per cent of your course costs of up to £200 (if your course costs more than this amount, you will have to pay the difference):

- Income Support;
- Jobseeker's Allowance (income based);
- Pension Credit;
- Housing Benefit;
- Working Tax Credit;
- Council Tax Benefit.

The money that you receive through the ILA will not affect the benefits that you receive.

If you are not claiming benefits and you do not have a qualification above Level 2, the ILA could pay 50 per cent of your course costs, up to £100. Again, if your course costs more than this amount you will have to pay the difference. To qualify you must not have qualifications any higher than the following:

- GCSE (grade A to G);
- GNVQ intermediate level;
- NVQ Level 1 or 2;
- GNVQ foundation level;
- BTEC first certificate.

If you are unsure about whether your previous qualifications will affect your eligibility for the scheme, you can telephone the ILA Wales team for advice on 0800 212134. If you find out that your previous qualifications preclude you from receiving this grant, you can download a publication called a *Guide to Funding* from the ILA website (details below). This describes the other types of funding that may be available for people living in Wales who wish to take part in further or higher education (see case study below).

Nerys found out about the ILA from a friend who had received some money to help to pay for some basic skills courses at the local college. After having been made redundant, Nerys wanted to study full-time at her local college to improve her skills and gain a vocational qualification that would help her to secure a job. However, when she applied for funding through the ILA scheme she found that she did not qualify because she had already gained two A Levels at school and because the course in which she was interested was a full-time course.

She was advised to look into the Assembly Learning Grant (ALG), which provides up to £1,500 for people from Wales who are on a low income. Because her income was below £5,745 at the time of application, Nerys received the full £1,500 grant towards her course. (Rules stipulate that, if applicants intend to study full-time, they must be following a post-compulsory education course of at least 500 hours a year, which leads to a nationally recognised qualification. If they want to study part-time they have to be studying at least 275 hours a year to qualify. Nerys intended to study for more than 500 hours in the academic year at an eligible institution and on a qualifying course and, therefore, received the full grant because of her low household income.) Nerys enrolled on her course and gained her qualification in June 2009. She is now actively seeking work.

Application procedure

If you need more information and guidance about which course to choose, contact Learning and Careers Advice or Careers Wales (details below). They have independent advisers who are able to offer advice about a variety of courses covering a range of subjects. They can also arrange for you to have a one-to-one discussion with a careers adviser who can help you to plan your career and further learning.

You can request an ILA application pack by telephoning Learning and Careers Advice (details below). Once you have returned your application form in the pre-paid envelope you will be set up with an account and will receive a welcome pack. This explains how you can use your account and provides information on the benefits of learning.

When you have found a suitable course take note of the start date and make sure that you can complete all the necessary paperwork before it commences. You will need to give your ILA Wales Reference to your learning provider and wait until you have received your course booking information letter from ILA Wales before you start your course.

Progression routes

Many people use their ILA account to try short, taster courses to help them to build their personal confidence in a learning environment. Some people will not have taken part in any formal learning since leaving school, and this grant provides the opportunity to try courses without spending too much of their own money. They find that learning as an adult can be both rewarding and fulfilling, and that the experience is nothing like they had encountered at school. If this is the case, you may find that you enjoy learning as an adult and want to continue, perhaps studying for a higher level qualification, or perhaps think about going to college or university in the future. More information about learning and earning schemes available in the further and higher education sectors are provided in this part of the book and in Part III.

Other people find that the confidence they gain on their course helps with their everyday life and that they are able to build social networks with people they have met on the course. You may decide that you want to continue learning for your own interest, because you enjoy what you have learnt and want to find out more, or your increased confidence may help you to apply for a new job or even set up your own business in the future.

Further information

Useful websites

www.ilawales.co.uk
Visit this site for information about the ILA in Wales. It provides information about the ILA, eligibility criteria and application procedures. There is also some interesting information on the benefits to be gained from returning to learning.

www.careerswales.com
Careers Wales is funded by the Welsh Assembly Government and is available to give free careers information, advice and guidance to people of all ages in Wales. Comprehensive information is available on all aspects of education, funding and hunting for jobs. The service is available in English and Welsh.

www.studentfinancewales.co.uk
Information about alternative sources of funding for students who wish to study at further and higher education in Wales can be obtained from this site.

Useful telephone numbers

Contact Learning and Careers Advice for information on ILA Wales-registered learning providers and to request an ILA application pack: 0800 100 900.

17 Individual Learning Accounts (Scotland)

The Individual Learning Account is a Scottish Government scheme to help people pay for the cost of learning. It is intended to encourage people who are on low incomes, or benefits, to take part in further learning. If you are aged 16 or over, live in Scotland and are earning less than £22,000 per year (2009 threshold) or are claiming benefits, this scheme may be of interest to you.

This chapter describes the Individual Learning Account (ILA) scheme in Scotland and provides information about the amount of money, the eligibility criteria, application procedures and progression routes, concluding with useful websites and contact numbers.

Type of scheme

This scheme provides you with an ILA that you can use for a wide variety of courses. It can be used for part-time study at colleges, universities or private training providers, for classroom-based, distance or online learning.

There are two types of account available (£200 and £500; see below) and the type that you choose depends on what you want to study. You can only hold one account at a time, so it is important that you choose the right one. If you need any advice to help you to make your decision you can telephone an adviser on the ILA helpline (details below).

Amount of money

There are two amounts of money available. First, £200 is available for people who meet the eligibility criteria who wish to improve their skills by learning something new. There is a wide variety of courses available and you can use the search facility on the ILA Scotland website to find a course in your area (details below). Examples of the types of subject that you could choose include computing, languages, counselling, fork-lift training and bookkeeping. You can study more than one course a year if you have not used all the money in your account. Funds cannot be carried over to the next year, but you can re-apply for the following year if your circumstances have not changed, and you will start afresh with £200 in your account.

Secondly, £500 is available for people who meet the eligibility criteria who are studying a part-time higher education course such as a Higher National Certificate (HNC), Higher National Diploma (HND) or a Degree course at ILA Scotland-approved colleges or universities. You must be studying 40 Scottish Credit and Qualifications Framework (SCQF) credits or more an academic year. Any higher education course at SCQF Levels 7, 8, 9 and 10 is eligible for this funding. Master's Degrees, Postgraduate Diplomas and Postgraduate Certificates (SCQF Level 11) will also be funded. More information about the SCQF and the qualifications within each level can be obtained from www.scqf.org.uk. You can reapply for funding every year that you are studying, as long as your circumstances haven't changed.

Eligibility criteria

To qualify for this scheme you must meet the following conditions:

- You must be ordinarily resident in Scotland (this means that you live in Scotland year after year by choice, apart from temporary or occasional absences such as holidays or business trips). If you are not a UK national, you must be settled in Scotland (as set out in the Immigration Act 1971) immediately before the date on which you made your application. More information about the residency criteria can be obtained from the ILA Scotland helpline (details below).
- You must have an income of £22,000 a year or less, or be on benefits.
- You must be aged 16 or over.

Application procedure

Visit the ILA Scotland website to apply online for an ILA, or phone the helpline below to request an application pack. You will be asked for some personal details and will be required to complete some basic questions to find out whether you are eligible for funding. Your application pack will be sent to you if you are eligible.

You will need to return the completed application form so that a full eligibility check can take place. If you are successful, it usually takes up to two weeks to process your application and open your account. If you have any problems with the application process you can use the helpline to speak to an adviser (details below). You will need to have received your ILA Scotland account number (available in your welcome pack) before you go ahead and book a course.

Progression routes

Many people use the £200 ILA to try taster courses to help them to build their personal confidence in a learning environment. Some people will not have taken part in any formal learning since leaving school, and this grant provides the opportunity to try courses without spending too much of their own money. You may find that you enjoy your learning experience and want to continue, perhaps studying for a higher level qualification, or you may decide that you want to continue your learning for your own interest, because you enjoy what you have learnt and want to find out more. If your circumstances haven't changed you can apply for an ILA each year to continue with this learning. Other people find that the confidence they gain on their course helps with their everyday life and that they are able to build social networks with people they have met on the course.

If you have taken advantage of the £500 ILA you may find that your new qualification enables you to apply for another job, for promotion with your existing employer, or to set up your own business. More information about applying for jobs can be obtained from the Careers Scotland website (details below) and more information about setting up your own business can be obtained from Business Link (www.businesslink.gov.uk). Alternatively, you may be interested in continuing your learning at higher education level and earning a wage. If this is the case there are a variety of schemes available that may suit your needs (see Part III).

Further information

Useful websites

www.ilascotland.org.uk
Visit this site for more information about Individual Learning Accounts in Scotland. The site contains all you need to know about the ILA, including eligibility criteria and a useful course search that enables you to search for a course by subject in your location. You can download an application pack for an ILA from the website.

www.careers-scotland.org.uk
This is the website of Careers Scotland where you can access comprehensive information about education, training and funding opportunities. There is also detailed advice on finding jobs, producing a CV and attending interviews.

Useful telephone numbers

To obtain more information about the ILA in Scotland, and to speak to a trained adviser, you can ring 0808 100 1090.

18 Adult Learning Grant (England)

The Adult Learning Grant (ALG) scheme was launched across England in 2007/08. Through this scheme eligible adults receive a weekly grant to help with their full-time studies. It is targeted at working people from low income families who do not have a Level 2 qualification. If you are over the age of 18 and wish to return to full-time study in England, this grant may be of interest to you.

This chapter describes the ALG scheme in England and provides information about the amount of money, the eligibility criteria, application procedures and progression routes, concluding with useful websites, contact numbers and further reading.

Type of scheme

The ALG provides money each week during term-time and is intended to help with course-related costs such as fees, books and other materials. For continued payment you will need to have satisfactory attendance on your course and your college will have to provide evidence each week that this is the case. Students who have received the EMA find the ALG a useful grant to obtain if they wish to continue with their studies when they are too old to qualify for the EMA (see Chapter 12 for more information about the EMA in England and see the case study below).

The grant is offered for a wide variety of subjects, ranging from child-care and retail to chemistry and maths. Contact your chosen college to find out whether the course in which you are interested is covered under the scheme.

Yes, it certainly helped me. I was really worried about still getting the EMA, 'cos that had really helped. So my tutor told me about this... It's lucky he knew 'cos I certainly didn't. So I applied and got it. Simple... I've only got one more year of the course but if I'd not got the money it would have been impossible. I work all hours as it is in the shop with me mum, at Morrisons. She got me the job there and I do nights... So the money really helped pay some extra and I didn't have to work every night. *Chris, 19, Weymouth*

Amount of money

The Adult Learning Grant is income-assessed and the amount you will receive depends on your family income. If you live with a spouse or partner who is in paid employment, you will receive the following amounts (2009 levels):

Household income	Weekly payment
Up to £20,817	£30
£20,818 – £25,521	£20
£25,522 – £30,810	£10
Over £30,810	£0

If you live without a spouse or a partner, or if your partner is not earning, you will receive the following amounts:

Household income	Weekly payment
Up to £11,810	£30
£11,811 – £15,405	£20
£15,406 – £19,513	£10
Over £19,513	£0

The grant is paid into your bank account each week during term-time. The ALG is normally paid for up to two years, but can be extended if you are studying for a first full Level 2 qualification and going straight on to a first full Level 3 qualification (and you expect to complete your learning within three years). Further information about the different levels of qualification is provided below.

Eligibility criteria

To be eligible to apply for the ALG you must meet the following criteria:

- You must be aged 19 or over.
- You must be intending to study full-time (at least 450 guided learning hours in any 12 month period or 150 guided hours per term).
- You must live in England and meet the residency criteria (details of this will be provided in the application pack).
- The course must lead to your first full qualification at Level 2 or 3. (Level 2 refers to a standard equivalent to five GCSEs at A–C level or an NVQ at Level 2. Level 3 refers to a standard equivalent to two A levels or an NVQ Level 3.) More information about levels of qualifications can be obtained from your chosen college or by visiting www. accreditedqualifications.org.uk.
- You must be studying on a course at a learning provider funded by the Learning and Skills Council (LSC). Check with your college to find out whether this is the case.

You will not be able to get the ALG if you are claiming 'out of work' benefits, which include the following:

- Jobseeker's Allowance;
- Income Support;
- Incapacity Benefit or Employment and Support Allowance.

However, other benefits, including most 'in-work' benefits, such as Working Tax Credit and Child Tax Credit, should not be affected by the ALG. Also, you will not be able to receive the ALG if you are in receipt of any of the following training allowances:

- Education Maintenance Allowance (EMA) (see Chapter 12);
- Apprenticeship payments (see Chapter 1);
- Train to Gain (see Chapter 10).

Application procedure

Application packs are available from colleges or from the Learner Support helpline on 0800 121 8989. When you find out about a suitable course ask for an Adult Learning Grant information pack and application form. Complete the form and return it to the address supplied so that your payments are not delayed. Retrospective claims can be made if you meet all the eligibility criteria and payments will be backdated to the start of the term in which you applied for the grant.

You will need the following when you make your application:

- a bank account that accepts electronic payments through the BACS system;
- a copy of your birth certificate, driving licence or current passport;
- evidence of your total taxable income and taxable benefits for the previous tax year, and that of your partner if you live with him or her.

Once you have returned your application with all the supporting evidence, your claim will be assessed. You will be notified of the outcome and if you are successful you will be told how much grant you will receive.

Progression routes

Many people use the ALG to undertake a course that will improve their job prospects. However, you may find that you enjoy your learning experience and want to continue, perhaps studying for a higher level qualification at college or university.

Other people find that, through increasing their qualifications, they are able to apply for a job, or apply for promotion with their existing employer. More information about all aspects of career planning and making job applications can be obtained from the government careers advice website (details below). Returning to learning can also help to improve job satisfaction and motivation levels, and increase personal confidence.

Further information

Useful websites

www.direct.gov.uk
Enter 'Adult Learning Grant' into the search box to be directed to the relevant pages on this government information website. Here you can find information about the ALG, including eligibility criteria and levels of funding.

http://careersadvice.direct.gov.uk
This website provides useful information on all aspects of jobs, careers and learning. You can use the tools available on this site to assess your skills and interests and help you to produce a CV that can be used when you apply for jobs.

Useful telephone numbers

More information about the ALG can be obtained from the Careers Advice Service: 0800 100 900.

Further reading

If you are an adult thinking about returning to learning you may find these books useful as these provide comprehensive information and advice for adults who may be unsure or unconfident about returning to a learning environment: Dawson, C E (2005) *Returning to Learning: A practical handbook for adults returning to education*, Oxford: How to Books (£9.99); and Dawson, C E (2006) *The Mature Student's Study Guide: Essential skills for those returning to education or distance learning*, Oxford: How to Books (£9.99).

19 City & Guilds Access Bursaries

The City & Guilds Group is a registered charity established in 1878 to encourage education and training in, and for, the workplace. It is the leading vocational awarding body in the United Kingdom, offering a wide variety of qualifications through approved centres worldwide. Qualifications can be gained in many sectors ranging from office-based and management qualifications to vehicle maintenance and hairdressing. City & Guilds offers a small number of bursaries for people who are finding it difficult to meet the costs of their course. If you are over 16, live in the United Kingdom and are interested in studying for a City & Guilds qualification, you may be interested in this scheme.

This chapter describes the City & Guilds access bursary scheme and provides information about the amount of money, the eligibility criteria, application procedures and progression routes, concluding with useful websites and contact numbers.

Type of scheme

Each year, City & Guilds offers a small number of access bursaries (educational grants) to individuals who wish to study for a City & Guilds, Hospitality Awarding Body (HAB) or National Proficiency Tests Council (NPTC) qualification. Information about these awarding bodies can be obtained from the City & Guilds website (details below). The bursaries can be used for the following purposes:

- to pay course fees if no other funding is available;
- to cover the cost of a break from work while you retrain;
- to help with childcare costs;
- to help with travel expenses;
- to pay for essential equipment or materials.

Only a small number of bursaries are awarded each year and competition can be strong (see case study below). If you are unsuccessful in your application, it is possible to study for your City & Guilds qualification while you are earning a full- or part-time wage, as the courses have been designed to fit around employment. For example, it is possible to study the following work-related qualifications through City & Guilds:

- National Vocational Qualifications (NVQs) (see Chapter 21);
- International Vocational Qualifications (IVQ);
- Scottish Vocational Qualifications (SVQs);
- single-subject diplomas;
- Apprenticeships and Modern Apprenticeships (see Chapters 1, 2, 3 and 4);
- higher level qualifications such as Higher Professional Diplomas (Level 4) and Master's Professional Diplomas (Level 7).

More information about all these qualifications and how they compare with other UK qualifications can be obtained from the City & Guilds website (details below). Most of the courses concentrate on building practical skills within the workplace, which means that the qualifications are respected by employers throughout the United Kingdom.

I had enrolled on a Certificate in Travel course which was a City & Guilds course I was going to study at Level 2. I've since also done the Level 3 and now I work as a travel agent in Bournemouth. I applied for the bursary from City & Guilds but I was not successful. They are quite hard to get. No one on my course got one, although not everyone applied. I was obviously working in a travel agents as a sales consultant while I was studying, so I did have a wage. But the problem was travel expenses I needed help with because when I first started there my wage was not brilliant. In the end I convinced my boss to help me out because she could see I was getting much better at the job. I am now a senior sales consultant and we are just enrolling another junior member of staff to do the same as me. I get quite a bit more pay now as well so that is great. *Jane, via e-mail, Bournemouth*

Amount of money

The amount of money varies, depending on your financial needs, your current financial circumstances and the number of bursaries already allocated. You can read case studies from people who have obtained bursaries in the past by visiting the City & Guilds website (details below). These give you an idea of how the bursaries have helped students to cover the costs of their courses over the years.

Eligibility criteria

To be eligible to apply for a bursary you will need to meet the following criteria:

● you must be aged 16 or over;
● you must be resident in the United Kingdom;
● you must be intending to study in the United Kingdom;
● you must be intending to study for a City & Guilds, HAB or NPTC qualification.

Application procedure

Fill in an application form obtained from the City & Guilds website (details below) and post it back using the freepost address provided. Applications are considered twice a year in June and December. If you miss the deadline for one of the closing dates your application will be carried over automatically to the next selection. If your application is successful you will be invited to attend an interview, for which your travel expenses are paid. Interviews are carried out at a number of centres throughout the United Kingdom and tend to last about 45 minutes.

Progression routes

City & Guilds qualifications are designed for the workplace and are recognised by employers throughout the world. Once you have obtained your qualification and updated your CV you will improve your chances of getting a job and you should be able to apply for more highly qualified positions. As you can undertake on-the-job training you may begin to enjoy your work more, with higher levels of personal confidence, motivation and job satisfaction. Many successful candidates also find that they are given extra responsibility by their employer.

Some people find that they enjoy their learning and wish to continue, perhaps by enrolling at a further education college or continuing to work towards a higher level of City & Guilds qualification. If you are interested in continuing with your learning, more information about the variety of learning and earning schemes that are available at further and higher education levels are provided in this part of the book and in Part III.

Further information

Useful websites

www.cityandguilds.com

This is the City & Guilds website, which has a section for people in the United Kingdom and a section for people in the rest of the world. You can find out more about the type of qualifications that are available and the subject areas that are on offer. The 'financial assistance' page provides more information about the access bursary and you can download an application form from this page.

Useful telephone numbers

More information about City & Guilds qualifications and the access bursary can be obtained by phoning 020 7294 2800.

20 Career Development Loans

If you want to study on a vocational course – that is, the course relates to your employment or your future employment prospects – you can apply for a Career Development Loan (CDL). The CDL programme is operated by the Learning and Skills Council (LSC) in partnership with three high-street banks: Barclays Bank, The Co-operative Bank and The Royal Bank of Scotland. You can apply for a CDL if you are employed, self-employed or unemployed.

This chapter describes the CDL scheme and provides information about the amount of money, the eligibility criteria, application procedures and progression routes, concluding with useful websites and contact numbers.

Type of scheme

A CDL is a personal loan between you and the bank that has been designed to help you to pay for work-related learning at further, higher or postgraduate level. The loans are intended to help with course fees, books, equipment, tools, childcare, travel expenses and living costs while you study. The LSC pays the interest on your loan while you are learning and for one month afterwards. You then repay the loan to the bank over an agreed period at a fixed rate of interest (this rate is agreed by you and the bank before you sign the contract, and can vary from bank to bank; see below).

Amount of money

You can borrow anything between £300 and £8,000 to help you to fund up to two years of study. This will be extended to three years if your course includes one year of relevant work experience. CDLs can cover up to 80 per cent of your course fees. However, if you have been out of work for more than three months the loan will cover all of your course fees. You can claim for living expenses only if these costs are not covered by any other grants or state benefits and you must not undertake work involving 30 hours per week or more.

Eligibility criteria

To be eligible to apply for a loan you must meet the following conditions:

- You must be 18 or over.
- You must be ordinarily resident in England, Scotland or Wales for a minimum of three months with an unlimited right to remain in the United Kingdom (you will not qualify for a CDL if your right to remain is subject to restrictions). Northern Irish students wishing to study in England, Scotland or Wales must also meet this condition. Northern Irish students studying in Northern Ireland do not qualify for a CDL.
- You cannot use a CDL for anything that is being funded by another source, such as a student loan or an NHS bursary.
- You must be unable to fund the course yourself. You will not be eligible for a CDL if you have 'reasonable or adequate access to funds to pay for the course yourself'.
- You must be intending to work in the European Union (or Iceland, Norway or Liechtenstein) when you have finished your course.

There is a variety of courses that are not eligible for a CDL. For example, you cannot receive a loan for a course that is based specifically on careers counselling or careers progression, such as CV writing, job-hunting and interview skills. You cannot use a CDL for a franchise course or a Foundation Degree. Ring the Career Development Information Line for further information about eligible courses (details below).

Application procedure

It is important to apply early for your loan. The application procedure can take up to four weeks and this may be even longer during busy months. Barclays and the Royal Bank of Scotland will accept applications three months before your course starts and the Co-operative bank will accept applications six weeks before. As you are applying for a loan that has to be paid back, you must make sure that this is the best route to take for your personal circumstances. Therefore, you should follow the steps outlined below if you want to apply for a CDL:

1. Make sure that the course is appropriate for your needs and that it will help you to achieve your aims. Will the qualification help you to progress in the way that you intend? Is the course of the right length and at a time and in a place that you can attend on a regular basis? If in doubt, discuss this with a trained careers adviser, either at your local college or by contacting the Careers Advice Service on 0800 100 900.
2. Make sure the learning provider is suitable. It is important to realise that neither the banks nor the LSC monitor or approve learning providers, even though the learning provider has to be registered. You need to make sure that it is a suitable place for you to study because you will still have to repay the loan even if you do not complete the course through no fault of your own.
3. Check that you meet the personal eligibility criteria (see above).
4. Check that your course meets the eligibility criteria (see above).
5. Work out how much you need to borrow. When you apply for a loan most of the banks will ask you to calculate your monthly living expenses. Also, they will want to know for how long you require the loan. You need to take into account expenses such as books, travel and equipment. If you think your previous credit history might be a problem you should discuss this with the bank before making your application. They will be able to offer advice about whether it is worth continuing with your application.
6. Choose a bank. Interest rates, application procedures and the length of time it takes to process applications vary from bank to bank. Obtain information from all three banks so that you can compare terms and conditions. Information can be obtained from your local branch or from the websites and telephone numbers listed below.
7. Complete and return the application forms to your chosen bank. Fill in the forms carefully, making sure that all information is included as this will help your application to run smoothly.
8. Await a response. The bank will contact you as soon as your application has been processed. If you are successful you will be sent a credit

agreement that you must sign and return. Your learning provider will be asked to inform the bank when you start your course and the money will not be released until the bank has received this confirmation. If your application has been unsuccessful you can try another bank.

Progression routes

CDLs can be used for a wide variety of courses, at further, higher and postgraduate level. Your progression routes, therefore, will depend on the level and subject of your course. For example, some people may use a CDL to fund a vocational course at their local college, which could lead to further learning or to employment. Some people may decide to use a CDL to fund a specialist postgraduate course in a subject such as management or business administration (see the case study below). This will enable them to apply for jobs within that specific subject area, or to apply for promotion with their existing employer, or set up their own business.

However, you must understand that the CDL is a loan that must be paid back, so you will need to make sure that you have the funds available to repay the loan, which will usually be from part- or full-time wages. It is possible to postpone the start of your repayments for up to 17 months if you are unemployed and claiming benefits or tax credits, or if you are receiving a training allowance, or have to extend your course due to ill-health or other special circumstances. If any of these situations apply to you, it is important to agree any postponement with your bank before your repayments are due to start.

I wanted to study a Master's Degree in Professional Development. The course was expensive and I couldn't pay all the money for the course fees, even in instalments, so I decided to take a gamble and take out a loan to pay for the course. I hadn't heard about Career Development Loans, but luckily my bank was Barclays and when I went to the bank manager he told me that I would be better applying for one of these loans as the interest rates might be better and, more importantly, I didn't have to start repaying the loan while I was on the course.

I wanted to do this Master's Degree because I was setting up my own business and I knew I would be able to develop my personal skills and for my consultancy work. I also thought it would give me more credibility. It was a gamble because I didn't know how my business would develop but luckily it has gone from strength to strength. I took the loan out in 2005, finished my course in 2007 and I've repaid all the money I owed. I probably would have still taken out a normal bank loan, although I've been told that some banks wouldn't have given me a loan because I didn't have a specific job, or a well-paid job. I don't know if this is right or not, but luckily I didn't have to worry about that because I got the Career Development Loan instead. *Christina, 39, via e-mail, Northampton*

Further information

Useful websites

www.direct.gov.uk

Enter 'career development loans' into the search box of this government information website to be directed to the relevant pages about CDLs. Here you can find all the information you require, including eligibility criteria, type of funding and repaying the loan. You can also book a free call-back from a CDL adviser or e-mail an adviser through this website.

Useful telephone numbers

For more information about CDLs, telephone the Career Development Loan Information Line on 0800 585 505 (the line is open Monday to Sunday, 8.00 am to 10.00 pm).

Alternatively, you can contact one of these three high street banks for more information: The Co-operative Bank: www.co-operativebank.co.uk (08457 212212); The Royal Bank of Scotland: www.rbs.co.uk (0800 121127); Barclays Bank: www.barclays.co.uk (0845 609 0060).

21 National Vocational Qualifications

National Vocational Qualifications (NVQs) are work-based qualifications available in England, Wales and Northern Ireland that are achieved through assessment and training. In Scotland they are called Scottish Vocational Qualifications (SVQ). If you are in paid or voluntary employment (full- or part-time), or you are at school or college with the opportunity for work placement, and you wish to improve your skills within your job, these qualifications may be of interest to you. NVQs can also be taken as part of an Apprenticeship (see Chapters 1, 2, 3 and 4).

This chapter describes NVQs and provides information about the amount of money, the eligibility criteria, application procedures and progression routes, concluding with useful websites and contact numbers.

Type of scheme

NVQs are based on a set of National Occupational Standards that describe the competencies or abilities expected in specific jobs. These reflect the skills and knowledge needed to do a job effectively, and show that you are competent in the area of work that the NVQ represents. They are offered at five levels, depending on the skills required for a particular job:

Level 1: you will need to show that you are able to apply your skills and knowledge in a range of activities related to your job, most of which may be routine or predictable.

Level 2: you will need to show that you are able to apply your skills and knowledge in a range of activities related to your job. Some of the activities will be complex or non-routine, and you may need to demonstrate that you can work on your own initiative and work well in a team or group.

Level 3: you will need to show that you are able to apply your skills and knowledge in a broad range of activities related to your job. Most of these tasks are complex and non-routine. There is considerable responsibility and autonomy, and control or guidance of others is often required.

Level 4: you will need to show that you can apply your knowledge and skills in a broad range of complex, technical or professional work activities performed in a wide variety of contexts and with a substantial degree of personal responsibility and autonomy. You may be responsible for the work of others and the allocation of resources.

Level 5: you will need to demonstrate your knowledge and skills in a wide and often unpredictable variety of situations. You will have a great deal of personal autonomy and often significant responsibility for the work of others and for the allocation of substantial resources. You will have to demonstrate the ability to analyse, diagnose, design, plan, execute and evaluate within your working role.

For more information about the various levels of NVQ, and to find out how these compare with other types of qualification, visit the Qualifications and Curriculum Authority website (details below).

There are over 1,300 different NVQs to choose from and they are available in the vast majority of business sectors, ranging from business and management to manufacturing, production and engineering. You can find a course near you by using the course search facility available at http://careersadvice-findacourse1.direct.gov.uk.

NVQs have been designed so that they can be taken at a pace that suits you. This means that there is no set timescale for their completion, although NVQs at Levels 1 and 2 tend to take around one year to complete, whereas NVQs at Level 3 may take around two years to complete.

NVQ assessment

Assessment is by a trained assessor, through observation, questioning, discussion and the creation of a 'portfolio of evidence' (this is a collection of evidence, such as examples of work, produced by you to prove your ability to do the job). The assessor will help you to undertake the following tasks:

- identify what you can already do in your job;
- agree what standard and level you hope to reach;
- analyse what you need to learn;
- agree what type of learning needs to occur, including where and how this learning will take place (for example, this could be in-house, with a training provider, at a local college or by distance or online learning).

Your employer may agree to provide you with other types of work, or more advanced levels of work, to help you to gain the evidence of competence you need.

Amount of money

Although there are no specific grants offered for NVQs, most people undertake the training while in paid employment, which means that they receive their usual wage, even while they are training. People who are not in receipt of a wage may be able to receive a training allowance from their work placement employer or from their learning provider. See Part I and elsewhere in this part of the book for the various training allowances that may be available if you wish to work towards an NVQ. For example, some people may choose to study for an NVQ as part of their Apprenticeship, and if they are not receiving a wage they may qualify for an EMA payment of £30 a week if they are aged 16–18; see Chapters 1 and 12 for more information about these schemes in England.

Eligibility criteria

There are no age limits or special entry requirements for NVQs. They can be taken if you are a full- or part-time employee, a voluntary worker or a school or college student with a work placement or part-time job that would enable you to develop the appropriate skills. However, you must be in some kind of work where you will have the ability to provide current evidence of your competence in your role.

Application procedure

If you want to work towards an NVQ you should speak to a trained adviser to find out whether it is the most appropriate option for your needs. If you are under 20 years old you can visit your local Connexions service or consult the Connexions website for more information (details below). Alternatively, consult the relevant careers advice website or ring the relevant helpline (details below). You should also discuss your plans with your employer, or careers staff at school or college, as they will be able to offer further advice about whether this is the most appropriate route and help you to decide at which level you should train.

If you decide that an NVQ is appropriate, you will need to complete an NVQ application form that will be available from your local college or training provider. You may be invited to an NVQ induction session, held in various locations throughout the county. The induction will provide you with more information on what is involved in completing an NVQ. You will then be assigned a personal adviser/assessor who will help you with assessing your needs and the production of your portfolio of evidence.

Progression routes

NVQs help you to improve your competence in your job. This means that you will be able to do your job more effectively and efficiently, and your employer may reward you for this by offering you more responsibility, increasing your wages, or through offering you promotion or the chance to work towards a higher level NVQ. People who have worked towards an NVQ in a voluntary job may find that they are able to secure full- or part-time employment as a result. Many people who have undertaken an NVQ find that their job satisfaction increases because they feel more confident and are able to complete the tasks required of them, and others decide to continue to a higher level NVQ, if their current employment enables them to do so.

If you are still at school or college you may find it easier to obtain a job when you finish your NVQ, perhaps with the employer through which you have received a work placement. In the current recession many people aged 18 to 24 are out of work. However, if you have work experience and NVQs you should stand a better chance of gaining employment when you leave school or college.

Further information

Useful websites

www.qca.org.uk
This is the website of the Qualifications and Curriculum Authority, which is the regulatory body for public examinations and publicly funded qualifications in England. Here you can find more information about all aspects of 14–19 education and training, GCSEs, NVQs, A levels, diplomas, work-related learning and the qualifications and credit framework.

www.sqa.org.uk
This is the website of the Scottish Qualifications Authority, which is the national body in Scotland responsible for the development, accreditation, assessment and certification of qualifications other than degrees. Here you can find further information about SVQs, Modern Apprenticeships and other types of education and training in Scotland.

www.connexions-direct.com
This is the website of Connexions Direct, which provides information and advice for people aged 13–19. In the 'learning' section of this website you can read more about NVQs. You can also find contact details of your local Connexions service, where staff will be able to provide more information about the qualifications and let you know whether they might be suitable for your needs.

http://careersadvice.direct.gov.uk
This website provides useful information on all aspects of jobs, careers and learning. You can use the course search tool available on this site to find out about the types of NVQs that are available in your area.

www.careers-scotland.org.uk
This is the website of Careers Scotland, which is part of Skills Development Scotland, Scotland's new skills body. On this site you can access contact details of your local Careers Scotland agency. You can also find information about SVQs and other qualifications that are available in Scotland.

www.careerswales.com
Careers Wales is funded by the Welsh Assembly Government and is available to give free careers information, advice and guidance to people of all ages in Wales. More information about NVQs is available on this site. The service is available in English and Welsh.

www.careersserviceni.com
The Careers Service Northern Ireland has been developed to offer advice and guidance on learning, training and employment opportunities in Northern Ireland. The website contains more information about all types of qualification in Northern Ireland, including NVQs.

Useful telephone numbers

Connexions Direct: 08080 013 219 (for people aged 13–19).
Careers Advice Service (England): 0800 100 900.
Careers Scotland helpline: 0845 850 2502.
Learning and Careers Advice in Wales: 0800 100 900.
Careers Service Support Unit (Northern Ireland): 028 9044 1781.

22 BTEC and OCR Nationals

BTEC qualifications and OCR Nationals are work-related qualifications, available in a wide range of subjects. They are usually studied at school or college on either a full- or part-time basis. These qualifications are mainly taken by learners over the age of 16, although some schools offer OCR Nationals at Levels 1 and 2 to 14- to 16-year-olds, normally in combination with other qualifications such as GCSEs or Key Skills. If you are interested in gaining qualifications while learning more about a particular sector or industry, these qualifications may be of interest to you.

This chapter describes BTEC qualifications and OCR Nationals and provides information about the amount of money, the eligibility criteria, application procedures and progression routes, concluding with useful websites and contact numbers.

Type of scheme

BTECs and OCR Nationals offer you the chance to study both theory and practice in a work-related subject that is of personal interest. Some of the courses may also involve an element of work experience. BTECs and OCR Nationals are not exam-based qualifications. Instead, you study real-life, work-based case studies and complete projects and assessments that contribute to achieving each of the units you study.

BTECs

BTECs are designed as specialist qualifications for students who have a clear view of their future career, or are seeking progression to higher education, or are hoping to improve their professional qualifications. They are available at the following levels on the National Qualifications Framework (NQF).

Level 1: BTEC Introductory Diplomas and Certificates (equivalent to GCSEs grades D to G);

Level 2: BTEC First Diplomas and Certificates (equivalent to GCSEs grades A* to C);

Level 3: BTEC Diplomas, Certificates and Awards (equivalent to A levels and recognised by universities and further education colleges for entry purposes);

Level 4: BTEC Professional Diplomas, Certificates and Awards (equivalent to HNCs and HNDs);

Levels 5 and 6: BTEC Advanced Professional Diplomas, Certificates and Awards (equivalent to various professional qualifications).

For more information about the NQF, and to find out how these qualifications compare with others, visit the Qualifications and Curriculum Authority website (www.qca.org.uk). More information about BTECs can be obtained from the Edexcel website (details below). You can use the BTEC National Centre Finder on this website to locate schools and colleges offering BTEC qualifications.

OCR Nationals

OCR Nationals offer an exam-free alternative to GCSEs and are available at Levels 1 to 3. All OCR Nationals help students develop their personal skills in areas relevant to the workplace, such as team-working, communication and problem-solving. The courses have been designed to accredit your achievements and ability to carry out tasks in a way that is relevant to the workplace (see case study below). For more information about OCR Nationals, visit the OCR website (details below).

Subject areas

BTECs and OCR Nationals are available in a wide range of subjects, including:

- public services;
- information technology;
- media;

- art and design;
- business;
- sport;
- science;
- health and social care.

Amount of money

Although there are no specific grants available to study for these qualifications, it is possible to learn while you earn in the following ways:

- Some people decide to work part-time while they are studying. This enables them to receive a wage and they find that the skills they are gaining on their course are useful in the workplace. Often, part-time employment of this nature can lead to a full-time position once you have completed your studies.
- If you are aged 16–19 you may be able to receive an Education Maintenance Allowance while you study (see Chapters 12, 13, 14 and 15).
- If you are over the age of 18, live in England and intend to study full-time, you may qualify for an Adult Learning Grant while you study (see Chapter 18).
- If you are studying for these qualifications as part of an Apprenticeship, you will be able to receive a training allowance (see Chapters 1, 2, 3 and 4).
- If you have children there are various support schemes and funds available to help you to find, and pay for, childcare while you are studying (see Chapter 23).
- Discretionary learner support funds are available throughout the United Kingdom to help students facing financial hardship. You may qualify for some of these schemes if you wish to study for BTECs or OCR Nationals (see Chapter 24).

Eligibility criteria

BTEC qualifications and OCR Nationals are available in all parts of the United Kingdom. You will usually need to be aged 16 or over to study for them (or you can be aged 14–16 to study for OCR Nationals at Levels 1 and 2; see case study below).

The qualifications you will require to be eligible to apply for a BTEC depend on the level at which you wish to study and the subject area. For example, if you want to study for a Level 2 qualification, you will generally need GCSEs grades D to G, or a Level 1 qualification in a similar subject. To study for a Level 3 qualification, you will normally need GCSEs grades A* to C, or a Level 2 qualification in a related subject.

For most OCR Nationals at Levels 1 and 2 you will not need any previous qualifications, but you may need some for Level 3. Check with your learning provider to find out whether this is the case.

Anna is attending a school in Northamptonshire that works towards OCR Nationals in ICT. She had the following to say about her course: 'Yeah, it's really good 'cos we got to do PowerPoint and we designed our own web pages and stuff which was really good. And we looked at other websites to say what was good and bad about them 'cos some are really rubbish and you just look at them and you know you can do better, like you know you can... I'd like to do that when I've finished at school, 'cos it's easy and I know I can do it, like we've already done it all at school.'

Application procedure

Applications are made through your chosen school or college and many will let you do this online. In most cases you will be required to complete a simple application form that can be done at any time of the year. Colleges will clearly display the dates by which your form should be returned.

For more advanced levels you may be required to attend an advisory interview to ensure that you are placed on the most suitable course and that the qualification is right for you. If so, you will be asked to complete an application form, attend an interview and provide examples of work, if relevant.

Progression routes

Since most BTECs and OCR Nationals have been designed in collaboration with the relevant industry, they can help you to gain the skills needed by employers. This will improve your prospects of obtaining work within your chosen sector when you have successfully completed your course. You may also receive a technical certificate that helps to prove to employers that you have the required skills to carry out the job efficiently. As mentioned in the Introduction, youth unemployment is rising during the current recession and qualifications of this nature should give you an advantage when you apply for jobs. Some courses involve an element of work experience, which will be useful to include on your CV when you are making your job applications.

Some people decide to continue with their learning after having studied for these qualifications. This could be at further or higher education level. BTECs and OCR Level 3 Nationals are eligible for UCAS tariff points. This is the system for allocating points to qualifications used for entry to higher education. It enables students to use a range of different qualifications, other than purely A levels, to help secure a place on an undergraduate course at college or university. The number of UCAS points awarded depends on the overall grade achieved. For more information about the tariff system, visit www.ucas.com. If you are interested in studying at university level, there are a number of bursaries and grants available. These are discussed in Dawson, C E (2009) *The Essential Guide to Paying for University: Effective funding strategies for parents and students*, London: Kogan Page (£9.99).

Further information

Useful websites

www.edexcel.com
This is the website of Edexcel, which is the awarding body for BTEC qualifications. On this site there is a section for students, which includes information about the qualifications that you can work towards. There is also some useful information on study options in the United Kingdom and overseas, along with tips on taking and passing examinations. You can use the BTEC National Centre Finder to locate schools and colleges offering BTEC Nationals in your area.

www.ocrnationals.com
This is the website of the awarding body for OCR Nationals. On this site you can find more information about the different levels of qualifications and view case studies about OCR Nationals. You can also access the 'career path finder', which lets you match careers with your OCR qualifications.

Useful telephone numbers

Careers Advice helpline: 0800 100 900.
Connexions Direct: 0808 001 3219.

23 Childcare Support Schemes

If you are hoping to learn and earn at the same time, and you have children, you may feel that your plans will be hampered by childcare costs. However, there is a variety of schemes available to help support learners who have children. If you are intending to return to learning, or retrain, and you have children, these schemes may be of interest to you.

This chapter describes the childcare support schemes that are available for training and study at further education level, for job seekers and for those who wish to continue their study into higher education. It goes on to provide information about the amount of money available, the eligibility criteria, application procedures and progression routes, concluding with useful websites and contact numbers.

Type of scheme

Further education

If you are interested in studying at further education level, there is a variety of schemes available to help you to pay for childcare, depending on your age and where you live and study. These are described below.

Care to Learn (England)

This is available for people with children, if they are under the age of 20, to help to pay for the cost of childcare while they are studying. You can study full-time, part-time, on short courses or take part in training such as Apprenticeships or e2e. For more information about the grant, visit www. direct.gov.uk and enter 'care to learn' in the search box.

Sixth Form College Childcare Scheme (England)

If you are a parent aged 20 or over and studying at a school sixth form or sixth form college, this scheme could help towards your childcare costs. You must be the main carer for a child under 15 years of age and be from a low income household. For more information about the grant, visit www.direct. gov.uk and enter 'Sixth Form College Childcare Scheme' in the search box.

Childcare Support Funds

There are various funds available through your college to which you can apply for help with the costs of childcare. Lone parents and young students with children may take priority when funds are allocated. The funds are discretionary, with no guarantee that you will be successful in your application. Speak to an adviser at your chosen college to find out what funds are available.

Discretionary learner support funds

These funds have been allocated to colleges (and universities) to help them to support students who may be facing financial hardship during their studies. They are available in all parts of the United Kingdom and can only be applied for direct from your college (or university) once you have enrolled on your course (they used to be called 'Financial contingency funds' in Wales, 'Access funds' in England and 'Hardship funds' in Scotland). Speak to an adviser at your chosen college (or university) to find out what funds are available and to find out whether you qualify for financial assistance from the funds. These funds are also available for other types of financial hardship (see Chapter 24).

Childcare fund (Scotland)

These funds are available to help cover the cost of registered childcare for students enrolling at further education colleges in Scotland. Priority is given to students facing financial hardship and to lone parents. Funds are limited, so contact your chosen college to find out what is available.

FE Awards (Northern Ireland)

You can apply for these awards to help you to cover the cost of childcare while you are studying. They tend to be allocated on a first come, first served basis, so you must apply early to your chosen college. More information about the funds can be obtained from your college.

Job seekers

If you are looking for work and you wish to improve your skills through education and training, there is some extra financial support available for childcare, as described below.

Jobseeker's Allowance

If you are claiming Jobseeker's Allowance you are eligible for childcare support while you are training. However, you need to make sure that the costs for childcare are paid directly by the training provider so they do not impact on your entitlement to benefits. More information about this support can be obtained from your learning provider.

New Deal for Lone Parents

Through this scheme you can access training courses for which all childcare costs are paid. To be eligible you will need to be a lone parent, not working, or working less than 16 hours a week (see Chapter 37 for more information about New Deal).

Free Childcare for Training and Learning for Work

This scheme is aimed at out-of-work parents with a partner who is in work, if their household income is below £20,000 (2009 figures). It is available for people who have one or more children aged 14 or under (18 or under if the child is disabled) to pay for Ofsted-registered childcare. For more information about the grant, visit www.direct.gov.uk and enter 'Free Childcare for Training and Learning for Work' in the search box. Applications are made through your learning provider.

Tax credits

If you are a part-time student and you have a part-time or vacation job, or you have children, you may be entitled to apply for tax credits. The Working Tax Credit and the Child Tax Credit were set up in April 2003 and have been designed to provide extra help for childcare and for working people on low incomes. Within the Working Tax Credit there is a childcare element that helps provide financial support for registered childcare.

The amount of tax credit you will receive depends on your family income, the number of children you have, their ages and whether or not they have any disabilities. You can obtain an estimate of how much you might receive by consulting www.taxcredits.inlandrevenue.gov.uk.

Higher education: England, Wales and Northern Ireland

If you have enjoyed your learning at further education level, and you wish to continue your learning into higher education, there are other grants that are available for childcare. These are discussed below.

Childcare Grant

This is available for full-time students in higher education with dependent children in registered or approved childcare. You cannot receive this grant if you or your partner are in receipt of the childcare element of the Working Tax Credit from HM Revenue and Customs. The Jobcentre Plus or Housing Benefit office should not take account of any payments you receive through this scheme. For more information about this scheme, consult the government information website (details below).

Parents' Learning Allowance

This is available to help with course-related costs for full-time students in higher education who have dependent children. It is available for those people who are in receipt of the Childcare Grant or for those with partners or spouses who are on a low income. The grant should not be taken into account when benefits are calculated. For more information about this scheme, consult the government information website (details below).

Higher education: Scotland

Lone Parents' Grant

This is available for single students bringing up children and covers 52 weeks from the first day of your course. More information can be obtained from the Student Awards Agency for Scotland (SAAS) website (details below).

Childcare Grant for Lone Parents

If you are in receipt of the Lone Parents' Grant, you may also qualify for an additional grant to help to pay for the cost of registered or formal childcare. More information can be obtained from the SAAS website (details below).

Childcare Fund

Your university may have a childcare fund that provides money for registered or approved childcare. You need to apply to your university as soon as possible as funds are limited. Contact them direct for more information about this fund.

Amount of money

The following amounts are based on 2009 levels.

- Care to Learn (England): This scheme pays up to £160 per child per week (£175 in London) to help with childcare costs.
- Sixth Form College Childcare Scheme (England): This scheme also pays up to £160 per child per week (£175 in London) to help with childcare costs.
- Childcare Support Fund: Amounts vary and depend on your financial circumstances and the amount of funds available. There is no guarantee that your application will be successful.
- Childcare in Scotland: Amounts vary, depending on your financial circumstances. Contact your chosen college or university direct for more information and advice.
- FE Awards (Northern Ireland): The FE Awards can pay up to 85 per cent of childcare costs, up to a maximum of £185 a week for one child and £300 for two or more children.
- Discretionary learner support funds: Amounts vary and depend on your financial circumstances and the amount of funds available. There is no guarantee that your application will be successful. Applications can only be made once you have enrolled on your course.
- Free Childcare for Training and Learning for Work: This scheme pays up to £175 per child per week (£215 per child per week in London).
- Childcare Grant (higher education): This scheme pays up to a maximum of £148.75 for one child and £255 for two children (England and Northern Ireland). In Wales the amounts are £161.50 per week for one child and £274.55 per week for two or more children. The money is paid in three instalments by the Student Loans Company (SLC) and is available during term-time and vacations.

- Parents' Learning Allowance (higher education): How much you get will depend on your income and that of your spouse or partner, up to a maximum of £1,508.

Eligibility criteria

Eligibility criteria vary, depending on the scheme. However, to qualify for any of the schemes you will need to have dependent children below the age of 19 and be from a low income household. For schemes administered by the SLC you will need to provide proof of your income when making your application. Discretionary funds may ask for additional supporting criteria, such as birth certificates.

Application procedure

To apply for Childcare Support Funds, hardship funds, the childcare fund in Scotland and the Free Childcare for Training and Learning for Work scheme, contact a student adviser at your chosen college or learning provider for an application form.

A Care to Learn application form can be downloaded from www.direct. gov.uk. You will need to take your child's birth certificate (or your Child Benefit letter) for your college to photocopy, and your childcare provider will need to submit a copy of their Ofsted registration certificate with your application. (The childcare provider must be on the compulsory part of the Ofsted Childcare Register or Early Years Register.)

If you are intending to enter higher education, you apply for financial support for childcare at the same time that you apply for other student financial support. Visit the relevant website listed below for more information and to make an application:

- Students in England: www.direct.gov.uk/studentfinance.
- Student in Scotland: www.student-support-saas.gov.uk.
- Students in Wales: www.studentfinancewales.co.uk.
- Students in Northern Ireland: www.studentfinanceni.co.uk.

Progression routes

Your progression routes will depend on the level at which you are undertaking your learning. It could lead to further education and training or help you to secure employment. Having your childcare paid for you while you study takes away some of the financial pressure and will enable you to concentrate on your studies so that you can progress successfully to further learning or employment.

Further information

Useful websites

www.direct.gov.uk
A copy of *A Guide to Childcare Grant and Other Support for Full-time Student Parents* can be downloaded from this government information website. You can also contact your Local Authority for a fact sheet called *Applying for the Childcare Grant – What you need to know*.

www.childcarelink.gov.uk
Visit this site for information about registered or approved childcare in your area.

www.entitledto.co.uk
This website provides a free web-based calculator to help people work out their entitlement to benefits and tax credits.

Useful telephone numbers

National Childcare Information Line: 0800 096 0296.
Call the Learner Support helpline for information about Care to Learn, Sixth Form College Childcare Scheme and the Free Childcare for Training and Learning for Work scheme: 0800 121 8989.

24 Discretionary Support Funds

For some people it is not possible and/or practical to earn a full-time wage while they are learning. Others find that a full- or part-time wage is not enough to see them through their studies. In these cases you may be concerned that your plans for further study will be hampered by financial constraints. However, there are discretionary support funds that are available for people who are finding it hard to meet the costs of taking part in further education at college or sixth form. If you are hoping to go to college or continue into sixth form, and you are not taking part in any of the work-based learning schemes described in Part I of this book, these funds may be of interest to you.

This chapter describes the discretionary support funds that are available for study at further education level, and provides information about the amount of money, the eligibility criteria, application procedures and progression routes, concluding with useful websites and contact numbers. Discretionary support funds are available in all parts of the United Kingdom, although schemes, amounts of money and eligibility criteria may differ slightly to those described below, so contact your chosen college for information specific to your region.

Type of scheme

Funds are available to help students who are facing financial hardship. They are intended to help with the following:

- Financial hardship and emergencies (these could occur at any time during your studies, and it is possible to apply for the funds at the time that you encounter the problem).
- Childcare costs for Ofsted-registered childcare. Costs tend to be awarded for timetabled hours: travel time between your college and your childcare

provider is considered when calculating childcare awards (see Chapter 23 for more information about funds for childcare).

- Accommodation costs for students who have to study further than the maximum distance from home and where a course is not available locally (this distance tends to be defined as more than 15 miles or a two-hour return journey).
- Costs for essential course-related equipment, books, materials and field trips.
- Travel costs, if you are over the age of 18. If you are aged 16–18 help with transport costs is available from your local authority, rather than through these funds. Use the postcode search facility on the government information website listed below to find out what help with transport costs is available in your area, or contact your local authority direct for more information.

You are able to apply for these discretionary support funds if you are in receipt of the EMA (see Chapters 12, 13, 14 and 15) or the ALG (see Chapter 18). You can also apply for these funds if you have obtained a Career Development Loan to help to fund your studies (see Chapter 20).

Amount of money

Funds are distributed by colleges and sixth forms, according to individual student need. Each applicant is assessed individually and the amount that you are awarded will depend on your financial circumstances and the amount of money that you need. To find out how much you could receive speak to your tutor, student support officer or welfare officer. Some funds, such as the childcare and residential funds, have maximum amounts available. In 2009 these maximum amounts were up to £160 per child per week (£175 in London) for childcare and up to £3,458 per year (£4,079 in the London area) for accommodation.

Some funds will be awarded as grants, which do not have to be paid back, whereas others may be awarded as loans that you will have to repay according to the terms of your agreement. Also, some of the funds will be paid direct to someone else, such as your landlord or your childcare provider. You must apply each academic year for funds to be awarded. The money is only released once you start attending your course.

You should note that funds are limited and may run out. No guarantee can be given that money will be available and if there is a high demand, funding for the spring and summer terms may be given at a reduced rate. Continued payment is also dependent on you achieving and maintaining satisfactory progress and attendance in all your classes.

Eligibility criteria

To be eligible for discretionary support funds you must be over the age of 16 (over the age of 18 for help with travel costs) and you must have been accepted onto and be studying a programme of learning funded by the Learning and Skills Council (LSC). Your college will be able to offer guidance about whether this is the case or not.

The funds are distributed by sixth forms and colleges themselves, so they are able to set additional eligibility criteria when allocating funds. The following types of student tend to take priority when funds are allocated:

- students who are economically disadvantaged (such as those from low income families or those in receipt of benefits);
- those aged over 19 who do not have a Level 2 qualification;
- students who have been in care or on probation, young parents and others considered at risk;
- students with disabilities and/or learning difficulties.

You are not eligible to apply for these funds if any of the following apply:

- you are under the age of 16;
- you are an asylum seeker aged over 19;
- you are receiving full public funding for higher education (including grants and loans);
- you are studying on a Learndirect course (these are online courses in basic English and maths and a range of courses in IT and business and management; visit www.learndirect.co.uk for more information);
- you are on a New Deal programme (except New Deal for Lone Parents: see Chapter 37);
- you are on an Apprenticeship training scheme (see Chapters 1, 2, 3 and 4);

- you are on a work-based learning course (see Part I of this book);
- you are on an Adult and Community Learning course (your learning provider will be able to offer advice about whether you are on this type of course).

You must remain eligible for an award throughout the duration of your course to receive continued payment, and you are expected to attend regularly in accordance with your timetable and make progress in your studies.

Application procedure

Applications are made through your sixth form or college once you have enrolled on your course. Contact your tutor, the student awards officer, the student support officer or the welfare officer for more information and to obtain an application form. Some colleges have the application forms available for download from their website.

You will have to provide documentary evidence of your financial circumstances when you make your application. This could include the following:

- wage slips for the last three months for those who are employed;
- forms from HM Revenue and Customs showing Child Tax Credit and Working Tax Credit payments, if appropriate;
- a letter dated within the last three months from Jobcentre Plus or the Department for Work and Pensions confirming the amount of any benefits you or your family receive;
- a Housing Benefit and Council Tax Benefit letter from your local council, if you receive either of these;
- bank statements for the previous three months.

Progression routes

If you choose to stay on at sixth form or college after you have completed your full-time education you will have the opportunity to apply for a wider variety of jobs, usually with higher wages, as a result of gaining more qualifications. According to the UK Commission for Employment and Skills (UKCES), those with tertiary (further education) level qualifications in the United Kingdom earn nearly 60 per cent more on average than those with secondary (school) qualifications, who, in turn, earn 30 per cent more than those with low/no qualifications. For more information, visit www.ukces.org.uk.

Also, you have the opportunity to continue your learning at university. If you are interested in studying at university, more information about learning and earning opportunities at higher education level is provided in the next part of this book. There are also a number of grants, bursaries and loans that are available for students from low income families and/or high achieving students; these are discussed in depth in Dawson, C E (2009) *The Essential Guide to Paying for University: Effective funding strategies for parents and students*, London: Kogan Page (£9.99).

Further information

Useful websites

www.direct.gov.uk
Enter 'discretionary support funds' in the search box of this government information website to find out more about the funds that are available.

http://lsf.lsc.gov.uk
More information about the discretionary support funds can be obtained from this LSC site. Information is provided on eligibility for the funds and there are some useful publications available for download.

Useful telephone numbers

If you are intending to study at a college away from home because the course you want is not available locally, you may be able to get financial help with the cost of your term-time accommodation. You can obtain a Residential Support Scheme application pack by phoning 0845 602 2260.

For information and advice on applications for discretionary learner support funds, the Education Maintenance Allowance (EMA), the Adult Learning Grant (ALG), Care to Learn, the Sixth Form College Childcare Scheme, Dance and Drama Awards and the Residential Support Scheme, phone the learner support helpline: 0800 121 8989.

Part Three

Learning and Earning in Higher Education

Balfour Beatty Construction Northern

A Management Career in Construction

The construction industry is the UK's largest single industry, responsible for employing over 2 million people and producing about 10% of overall GDP.

Construction is very intellectually demanding as it is a complex process but the satisfaction of seeing your project completed and leaving your mark on the world is second to none.

Any construction project relies on a wide range of skilled people across several phases. The significant phases are as follows:

Concept and design – this is undertaken by an Architect, usually assisted by a Structural Engineer, who works with the client to translate their aspiration into a design. Companies need to ensure that the design is practical to build and the costs and timescales are realistic.

Selection of the construction team – the client selects a team to build their project from a number of tenders, using criteria such as reputation, skills, creativity and price. They are assisted by a team of consultants, who help to determine the budget and the outline programme. Companies have teams of staff who work on tenders to ensure that they win plenty of projects for the future.

Construction – different parts of the project are built by specialist contractors – such as groundworkers, steel erectors, bricklayers, carpenters, electricians, decorators etc. The main contractor's job is to manage them through selecting the most appropriate contractor, plan the timescales involved, sequence them correctly, monitor their progress whilst on site and solve any problems. Throughout the project the main contractor must brief the client, stick to the budget, motivate the various teams and ensure that all activities are conducted safely.

Ongoing maintenance and repair – once a building is completed, specialist companies are responsible for ensuring that it works to its maximum efficiency throughout its lifecycle.

Working for a main contractor

Balfour Beatty Construction is a main contractor which manages specialist contractors to ensure that a project is completed safely, on time, to budget and to the customer's quality standards.

As a UK-wide company we specialise in the construction of new buildings including hospitals, schools, offices and retail parks – ranging in value from half a million pounds to half a billion!

Examples of current projects include:

- The new Queen Elizabeth Hospital in Birmingham
- Northern Batch Hospitals'
- Manchester Schools

Most employees are based on construction sites across the UK, with some working from regional offices (Manchester, Newcastle, Leeds and Birmingham).

Balfour Beatty are at the forefront of the latest developments in construction – including safety, environment and sustainability, radical forms of project finance, innovative management techniques or new technology.

Overall turnover is around £450 million with 690 employees across the UK. Balfour Beatty Construction Northern are part of the Balfour Beatty Group, the UK's largest construction, engineering and services company with an overall turnover of £9.5 billion and 40,000 employees.

The job roles

There are a number of different professional and managerial roles that you can aspire to become:

Design Managers manage the architects and ensure that their designs are safe and easy to build, meet the client's requirements in terms of user criteria, environmental performance, cost and timescale. They also act as a link between the architect and construction teams and ensure that everybody has the correct information in the right place at the right time.

Engineers are responsible for ensuring that the building is constructed with the correct level of dimensional accuracy and that specialist contractors are properly briefed and supervised.

Estimators work on tenders to predict the cost of the building that the client requires and discusses costs with potential specialist contractors.

Planners work out how long the different construction activities will take and so predict how long a project will take to complete and what resources will be required.

Project Managers are responsible for the project from start to finish and manage the site teams. They speak directly to the client throughout the project and ensure that the client is fully aware of the progress. The buck stops with the project manager!

Site Managers control the site itself, ensuring that the specialist contractors are co-ordinated, materials and plant are delivered and stored correctly, potential problems are solved in advance and that all activities are carried out safely.

For any of these roles a degree in a built environment subject is essential; this will give you not only the required underpinning knowledge but also provide you with the baseline for going on to become professionally qualified.

You can either go to university full-time and gain work experience during summer placements and a year out, alternatively you can study for the same degree on a part-time basis attending university one day a week.

Balfour Beatty Construction Northern Case Study

Adele Armitage – Trainee Quantity Surveyor

I always wanted to work in a job that I could be constantly learning new things, meeting new people and challenging myself.

I have been very lucky in my role as a Trainee Quantity Surveyor with Balfour Beatty as the first project I am working on is the new acute Pinderfields Hospital in Wakefield with a project value of £200million.

Working for Balfour Beatty on this project provides me with new, exciting and rewarding challenges everyday.

My role involves preparing new Sub contracts, measuring progress, reviewing and preparing payment certificates, making sure accurate and detailed records are kept as well as making regular visits on to the site to generally learn the construction process.

Balfour Beatty has given me the opportunity to combine my every day work with a day release programme at Sheffield Hallam University. The work is hard and sometimes it feels that there just aren't enough hours in the day, but with the support I have received from all my colleagues I am proud to say I have gained my HNC in Building Studies and this year I will be starting my degree in Quantity Surveying.

My ambition is to go on with Balfour Beatty get my degree and become a fully qualified Quantity Surveyor with RICS accreditation.

I really enjoy all aspects of my role and training and would recommend it to anyone.

The debt-free degree

Want a degree but don't want the debt? Gain debt free degree and a well-paid and challenging job with excellent career development opportunities with Balfour Beatty.

It will take you five years to obtain your degree on a day release basis – only a year longer than a full time sandwich degree – and you will spend the other four days in the workplace, following a structured and accredited on-the-job training scheme.

These are permanent jobs with education and training attached so on completion of your degree you will continue your career by becoming chartered with one of the major construction industry professional bodies and moving up the management ladder.

Training pathways

Site Management – you will start off in an engineering role, before moving into site supervision and then site management. Support will be given for a degree in Civil Engineering or Construction Management.

Design Management – you will assist the design managers in the flow of design information, as well as spending time on site in an engineering role and in an architects office understanding the design process. Support will be given for a degree in Architectural Technology or Construction Management.

Commercial Management – working as a junior quantity surveyor, you will select and monitor specialist contractors, control costs and ensure legal compliance. Support will be given for a degree in Quantity Surveying or Construction Management.

Whichever pathway you choose, as well as your degree you will receive intensive on the job training leading to NVQs at levels 3 and 4, technical and managerial training and regular safety training. Once you have finished your degree, your training will focus on becoming a Chartered Builder, Engineer or Surveyor.

Entry requirements

You will need A-levels/Highers/AVCE with at least 260 UCAS points or an HNC/D in a built environment subject.

Recruitment process

All applications must be made online. To see vacancies and apply, please visit the Balfour Beatty Construction Website: www.bbcl.co.uk

Useful websites:

www.balfourbeatty.com – Balfour Beatty Group

www.bconstructive.co.uk – Careers in Construction

www.constructionskills.net – Sector Skills Council

www.cstt.org.uk – Chartered Surveyors Training Trust

www.ciob.org.uk – Chartered Institute of Building

www.ice.org.uk – Institute of Civil Engineers

www.rics.org.uk – Royal Institution of Chartered Surveyors

25 Part-time Learning and Earning

The previous part of this book has discussed the different schemes that are available for people who want to learn and earn in the further education sector. This part now moves on to look at the learning and earning schemes that are available in the higher education sector.

This chapter discusses the different learning opportunities that are available for people who want to continue their learning at higher education level while they are earning a wage in full- or part-time employment. This includes open and distance learning, part-time courses, foundation degrees, credit accumulation and transfer, and the accreditation of prior learning. It goes on to discuss the amount of money that may be available for this type of learning, eligibility criteria, application procedures and progression routes, concluding with useful organisations, useful websites and further reading.

Type of scheme

'Higher education' refers to education carried out at a level higher than A levels or Level 3. For information about the different levels of qualifications available in England, Wales and Northern Ireland, visit the Qualifications and Curriculum Authority website (www.qca.org.uk). If you live in Scotland, visit the Scottish Qualifications Authority website for information about the different levels of qualification that are available in Scotland (www.sqa.org.uk).

Higher education courses tend to be delivered in universities or colleges of higher education, although some further education colleges and adult residential colleges may offer some higher education courses, such as foundation degrees or the first year of an honours degree course. For a list of learning providers offering courses at higher education level, visit the Universities & Colleges Admissions Service (UCAS) website (details below).

If you want to learn while you earn at higher education level there are various routes that you can choose, described below.

Open and distance learning

With the rapid growth in the development and use of information technology, open and distance learning (ODL) has become a popular method of study, especially for those adults who want to learn while they earn. ODL includes any learning provision in which a significant part of the learning is managed by the learner, and ranges from online learning to traditional correspondence courses. Many universities and other learning providers offer the opportunity to study for a degree or postgraduate qualification through ODL. This enables you to continue working full- or part-time, fitting your studies around your working hours at a time that suits you. These courses employ a variety of teaching and learning methods, such as online tutorials, individual activities, assignments and online conferencing.

If you are interested in this type of learning, ODL courses require a specific set of skills from the learner, such as the ability to learn as an individual without face-to-face contact; the need to build and maintain motivation without the support of other students; and the ability to meet deadlines without constant reminders from tutors. ODL students must learn how to use a variety of self-instructional media and print materials, and they need to be organised and self-disciplined. If you believe you have these attributes, and you are interested in this type of learning, ODL can provide a useful way to learn and earn at the same time.

You should be aware that there are some bogus and unscrupulous companies offering distance learning courses at extortionate rates, usually leading to qualifications that are not recognised by employers or educational establishments. Make sure that the university/college you choose is accredited by the Open and Distance Learning Quality Council (www.odlqc.org.uk). If you are interested in a European ODL course, visit the European Association for Distance Learning website for more information and advice (www.eadl.org). You can also check that a learning provider is legitimate by visiting the UK Register of Learning Providers (www.ukrlp.co.uk).

When choosing an ODL course you need to make sure that you understand the costs involved, which could include tuition fees, examination/assessment fees, enrolment/registration fees and any additional money

you may need to spend on IT equipment, books and stationery. More information will be available from the prospectus and course tutor.

The Open University

The Open University (OU) is perhaps the best known provider of distance learning at higher education level. It was founded 'to bring higher education to people who are unable to study at a conventional university'. Most students study part-time with over 70 per cent of students working full-time during their studies. The OU offers over 580 courses and for many of them you do not need any specific entry requirements, although you will need to make sure that you study on a course at the appropriate level. More information about courses, qualifications, entry requirements and prices can be obtained from the OU (details below).

Part-time courses

Some people prefer to study in tutorials, seminars and lectures at a university or college as they enjoy the social interaction and learning environment. All universities offer part-time courses for students who wish to study in this way, and these courses will be available at times when people in employment can study. For example, some courses may be offered in the evening, perhaps on a weekly basis, whereas others may be offered on day or block release. If you are hoping to study at your local university, contact them direct for a prospectus of part-time courses. This will contain all the information you require, including details of courses, qualifications, eligibility, application procedures and prices. Alternatively, you can use the part-time course search facility available at www.hotcourses.com to find a part-time course suitable for your needs.

Foundation degrees

Foundation degrees were set up by the Higher Education Funding Council for England (HEFCE) with what was then the Department for Education and Skills (DfES) in 2001–2. They were designed as a new two-year higher education qualification that could be completed quicker than a conventional degree, especially for people who were reluctant, or unable, to take too much time from work for their studies. (The DfES has been replaced by the Department for Children, Schools and Families (DCSF) and the Department for Business, Innovation and Skills (BIS).)

Foundation degrees are offered by universities in partnership with higher and further education colleges and have been designed to give people the technical and professional skills that are in demand by employers. They combine academic study with workplace learning and take two years to complete on a full-time basis or three to four years on a part-time basis. There are hundreds of courses available, covering a diverse range of subject areas, and study methods are flexible to enable people in work to fit their studies around their work commitments. There are no set entry requirements for these degrees: staff at the university that you choose will decide whether you are eligible and will take into account your previous work experience (see below). You can use the search facility at http://fd.ucas.com to find a foundation degree suitable for your needs.

Foundation degrees may be of interest to you if you wish to continue in part- or full-time employment while you are studying. They can be directly related to your work, which will help you to carry out your work more effectively and efficiently, or they could be in a different subject that may help you to change careers at a later date. They can also be of interest to people who are seeking work, as they provide the opportunity to study on a vocational course that will enhance your chances of finding work, or enable you to transfer to a full degree course if you enjoy, and succeed in, your studies.

Credit accumulation and transfer system

The credit accumulation and transfer system (CATS) has been designed to enable students to build up credits towards their final qualification (such as a certificate, diploma or degree) over a period of time. This means that you can take modules for a course when you have the time and finances to do so, dipping in and out of your learning when it suits you. It also means that you can take different modules at different universities and that you do not have to follow a specific, predefined course of study. Credits are awarded for each module that you study through the achievement of learning outcomes and their assessment. They can also be awarded for your prior learning (see below). The amount of credit that you achieve is related to the amount of learning that you undertake. In most universities learning is in the form of modules of 10, 15, 20 or 30 credits and the smallest unit of learning will be 10 credits.

For more information about CATS, visit the relevant credit framework website (details below). These websites contain useful information about the number of credits that you can receive for the type of learning you undertake. It is also possible to equate CATS with the Scottish Credit and Qualifications Framework (www.scqf.org.uk) and European Credit Transfer and Accumulation System (ECTS), which means that you can build up credits on courses at a wide variety of European universities. For more information about gaining credits in Europe, visit the European Commission Education and Training website (http://ec.europa.eu/education).

Accreditation of prior learning

In addition to credits that you obtain on your course, it is possible to build up credits towards your final qualification through the recognition of your prior learning. This can be known as Accreditation of Prior Learning (APL) or Accreditation of Prior Experiential Learning (APEL). Through this procedure your learning that has been achieved outside formal education through life and work experiences is identified and assessed so that credit can be awarded. It is important to note, however, that it is what you have learnt from your experience, rather than the experience itself, that is assessed. Increasingly, universities are considering assessing learning in part-time employment that takes place alongside your formal studies, which is very useful for those who wish to earn and learn at the same time. More information about APL and APEL can be obtained from the credit framework websites listed below.

APL and APEL can also be used for entry into further education, adult education and higher education, perhaps if you do not have any formal qualifications or qualifications at the level required for the course. They are of particular use for vocational courses that are relevant to the work that you have done in the past or to work that you are undertaking while you study. You will need to identify your prior learning and submit evidence that can be assessed when you make your application. More information about this procedure can be obtained from your tutor.

Amount of money

If you choose to learn while you are in full- or part-time employment, you will receive your usual wage while you are learning. Some employers may provide paid time off for study, especially if your learning will help you to carry out your job more effectively and efficiently.

In addition to your wages, there are various schemes available to help you to pay for study at higher education level, as detailed below.

Financial help with tuition fees and course costs

If you are thinking about studying part-time, fees vary considerably so you will need to contact the university in which you are interested to find out more about their course fees. As a general guide fees tend to range from £300 – £600 for a 15 or 20 credit unit. As a part-time student you can choose how many units you wish to take a year and there is some government funding available to help you to pay for the course, depending on the intensity of your study.

In England and Northern Ireland there is a fee grant of up to £1,210 per year from the government for part-time students who are studying at a rate of 50 per cent or more of a full-time equivalent course (2009/10 figures). The amount you will receive is based on family income and is linked to the intensity of study. Part-time students in England and Northern Ireland can also receive a grant of up to £260 per year, based on household income, to help with course-related costs. In Wales the amount that you can receive depends on the intensity of your study up to a maximum of £955 (2009/10 figures). You can also apply for financial help towards course-related costs, up to a maximum of £1,075. In Scotland you may be eligible for a fee grant of up to £500.

You should note that, if you wish to accredit your prior learning, institutions usually charge a fee for the administration of accrediting experience, so you will need to find out how much your chosen institution charges for doing this.

Financial help for childcare and dependants

Part-time and ODL students with dependants in England, Wales and Northern Ireland may be eligible to apply for additional support through the Part-time Childcare Grant, Part-time Adult Dependants' Grant and Part-time Parents' Learning Allowance (similar schemes are available in Scotland). The amount of support you may be eligible to receive will depend on your household income and the intensity of study on your part-time course.

Further information about financial support for childcare and dependants can be obtained from the relevant student finance website (details below).

Financial support for people with disabilities

The Disabled Students' Allowances (DSAs) are funds set up by the government to help you with extra costs you may have to pay as a result of your disability. The funds will pay for non-medical personal help, major items of specialist equipment, travel and other course-related costs. DSAs are not dependent on your income or that of your parents and are available for full- and part-time study. A booklet called *Bridging the Gap* answers most questions about DSAs and can be downloaded from the relevant student finance website (details below).

Career development loans

CDLs provide a loan to help cover the cost of course fees, up to £8,000, and may be available for part-time study at higher education level, depending on the type of course (see Chapter 20).

Benefits

If you intend to study part-time and you are on a low income, you may be eligible to claim some benefits as the part-time financial support described above is not considered to be enough to affect your entitlement. However, you should check with your Jobcentre Plus office to be sure. The benefits that you could claim include Income Support, income based Job-Seekers Allowance, Disability Living Allowance, Incapacity Benefit, Maternity Benefit, Housing Benefit and Council Tax Benefit.

University bursaries

Since the introduction of variable tuition fees in England, Wales and Northern Ireland in 2006 all universities intending to charge the higher fees must have a bursary scheme in place to help students from low income families. Each university must produce an Access Agreement that provides details of their bursary scheme. These Access Agreements can be obtained from www.offa.org.uk or from individual university websites.

Some universities only have bursaries available for full-time students, paying the full fee. However, a minority of universities have included part-time students in their Access Agreements, so this could be a useful source of income for your studies, depending on where you decide to study. Contact the university in which you are interested for more information about whether you might qualify, or see further reading below. Alternatively, you can access the bursary map available at http://bursarymap.direct.gov.uk to find out what bursaries are available from universities in England.

Eligibility criteria

Universities will set their own eligibility criteria for courses, so you will need to contact them direct to find out whether you are eligible to enrol. For some vocational courses, such as foundation degrees, admissions staff may look favourably on your previous work experience, rather than rely on your previous qualifications (see APL and APEL, above).

If you are hoping to obtain financial support for your studies, in most cases you will need to be from a low income family, in receipt of benefits or tax credits, or have a disability and/or dependants. You will have to provide proof of your financial circumstances when you apply. For information about the specific eligibility criteria for the different types of grant available for study at higher education level, visit the relevant student finance website (details below).

Application procedure

Applications for part-time study are made direct to the university in which you are interested. You will need to complete an application form and provide proof of previous qualifications and work experience, if relevant. In some cases you may also need to attend an interview. Currently there are moves towards having all part-time course applications made through the Universities & Colleges Admissions Service (UCAS), the organisation responsible for managing applications to full-time higher education courses in the United Kingdom. If you are interested in studying on a full-time course at university, including a full-time foundation degree, applications are made through UCAS. For more information about the application procedure, contact UCAS (details below).

Applications for financial support are made through the relevant student finance website (details below) or you can obtain further information from the student finance section of your local authority. Applications for the part-time fee grant in Scotland can be made by contacting ILA Scotland on 0808 100 1090. More information about all aspects of financial support for university study can be found in *The Essential Guide to Paying for University* (details below).

Progression routes

Studying for a certificate, diploma, degree or postgraduate qualification should enhance your career prospects and earning potential significantly. (A recent study by the Association of Graduate Recruiters reports that the average starting salary for graduates is £25,000.) It will also help to increase your self-confidence, personal satisfaction and self-esteem, help your intellect and knowledge base to grow, increase your analytical skills, and develop your transferable skills, which can be used to help you succeed in a wide variety of careers and life experiences. It will increase your social circle and help you to network on a personal and professional level.

If you choose to study a foundation degree there is the opportunity to progress to a full honours degree with just a further 12–15 months of full-time study or a slightly longer period of time if you choose to study part-time. Foundation degree graduates can also progress on to further professional qualifications. The study that you undertake on your foundation degree can be directly related to your full- or part-time work, which should help to improve your skills and efficiency, and increase your personal motivation.

Further information

Useful organisations

If you are interested in finding out more about courses offered by the Open University, you can contact the OU at the following address:

The Open University
Student Registration & Enquiry Service, PO Box 197,
Milton Keynes MK7 6BJ
Tel: (0845) 300 60 90; e-mail: general-enquiries@open.ac.uk;
website: www.open.ac.uk

If you want more information about applying for full-time courses at
university in the United Kingdom, contact UCAS:

UCAS
Customer Service Unit, PO Box 28, Cheltenham GL52 3LZ
Tel: (0871) 468 0 468; e-mail: enquiries@ucas.ac.uk;
website: www.ucas.com

Useful websites

For more information about all aspects of financial support for students,
visit the relevant student finance website:

England: www.studentfinanceengland.co.uk
Wales: www.studentfinancewales.co.uk
Northern Ireland: www.studentfinanceni.co.uk
Scotland: www.saas.gov.uk

www.findfoundationdegree.co.uk
More information about foundation degrees can be obtained from this
site, and there is a useful course search facility to help you find a foundation degree course that is suitable for your needs. You can search by category (which gives you a broad listing of courses available), or you can
search by region and/or course title. The site also contains useful information for employers and course providers.

www.nuccat.ac.uk
This is the website of the Northern Universities Consortium for Credit
Accumulation and Transfer (NUCCAT), which is a federation of some 40
higher education institutions in the United Kingdom. On the website you
can find more information about work-related learning and credits in
higher education.

www.nicats.ac.uk
This is the website of the Northern Ireland Credit Accumulation and Transfer System (NICATS), which is a credit framework for valuing, describing, measuring and recognising all learning. More information about this system, including a useful FAQ section, can be obtained from this site.

www.hefcw.ac.uk
This is the website of the Higher Education Funding Council for Wales. If you want to know more about achieving credits at university in Wales, enter 'Credit and Qualifications Framework for Wales (CQFW)' to be directed to the relevant section of this website.

www.seec.org.uk
This is the website of the Southern England Consortium for Credit Accumulation and Transfer. SEEC is a registered charity that was formed in 1985 and was the first higher education consortium for credit accumulation and transfer (CATS) in the United Kingdom. On this site you can find more information about credits in higher education and information about accrediting your prior learning.

Further reading

If you want to find out more about university bursary schemes, you may find Dawson, C (2009) *University Tuition Fees and Bursary Schemes, 2009/10* useful, as it contains comparative tables of all universities in England, Wales and Northern Ireland. It lists the amount of tuition fee charged, amount of bursary available, eligibility criteria, application procedure, contact details and other sources of funding that are available from each university. Information about this book can be obtained from www.studentcash.org.uk.

If you are thinking about studying at higher education level and you want to know more about the financial support that is available, you may find Dawson, C (2009) *The Essential Guide to Paying for University: Effective funding strategies for parents and students*, London: Kogan Page (£9.99) useful; it provides comprehensive advice and guidance about funding your university studies.

26 Vacation and Term-time Work

Some students find that the best way to learn and earn while in higher education is to enrol on a full-time course and earn money on a part-time basis, perhaps during term time, during the vacations, or both. If you are thinking about enrolling on a full-time higher education course and you would like to earn while you study, there are various options available to you, such as evening jobs, university jobs or vacation work.

This chapter describes the type of work available to you while you study, and includes information about the level of wages, the eligibility criteria, application procedures and progression routes, concluding with useful websites, useful telephone numbers and further reading.

Type of scheme

Research by the National Union of Students (NUS) suggests that over 90 per cent of UK-based students work in paid employment during the vacations, with between 40 and 70 per cent working in paid employment at some time during the term-time. Some students prefer to work only during the vacation, saving money to see them through the term, whereas others find it more convenient to work during term time. Others, usually due to financial necessity, work both during vacations and term, often obtaining a full-time position with the same employer when they are not studying.

University jobs

Over half of all employed students obtain jobs working for the university. This is because it is more convenient to work close to where they study and because university employers are more sympathetic to the needs of student employees. The following jobs are commonly available on university campuses throughout the United Kingdom:

- bar work, in students' union and university bars;
- glass collectors for students' union events, university events and outside events;
- waitresses/waiters for students' union or university restaurants, canteens and cafés;
- cooks/chefs;
- cleaners for halls of residence, offices and teaching rooms;
- administrators for the student finance office or the student accommodation office;
- tour guides for new students, school parties, prospective students and parents;
- note-takers for students with a hearing impairment or other relevant disability;
- mentors for new students or those experiencing learning difficulties;
- demonstrators for science subjects;
- research assistants;
- research participants (for online surveys, focus groups or drug testing, for example);
- receptionists (for special events, departments or schools);
- security personnel, usually at entertainment events.

Non-university jobs

Popular jobs for students away from the university tend to be in offices, pubs, cafés or restaurants. Some students work for call centres, finding work in this sector desirable as the hours are flexible with plenty of evening and weekend work available. Also, for those who are good at what they do, incentives and bonus schemes can mean that wages are increased considerably.

Student employment services

Many universities have set up their own employment services to meet the demand for student employment. It is estimated that these employment services now provide access to working opportunities for over 120,000 students a year. Contact details of all these services can be obtained from the National Association of Student Employment Services (NASES) website (details below). Advisers in the employment services liaise with employers in the local area and advertise opportunities in their offices, via a newsletter and/or e-mail to individual registered students. However, the employment services are not agencies, so you will have to liaise with each prospective employer, apply for the job and be paid by the employer.

Many employment services have made an agreement which means that, as a student, you can access the services of another college or university to find employment. This is useful if you study away from your home town but wish to find vacation work when you return home.

Working hours

The number of hours you decide to work is usually your own decision and will depend on how much time you can spare and how much money you need to earn. However, some universities have regulations about the number of hours a week you are able to spend in paid employment during term time if you are a full-time student. These limits are an attempt to make sure that your employment does not have a detrimental impact on your studies. If you are thinking about obtaining a job you should find out whether your university has such regulations. Visit your students' union, student finance office or university employment service for more information.

Amount of money

The National Minimum Wage (NMW) is a minimum amount per hour that most workers in the United Kingdom are entitled to be paid, and this includes students who are undertaking part-time and vacation work. However, you should note that if you are a student doing work experience as part of your higher or further education course you are not entitled to the NMW if the work experience does not last longer than a year (see Chapter 27 for more information about work experience and placements). If you are unsure about your entitlement to the NMW, and you are being paid less than the amounts listed below, you should contact your student union or university employment service for advice. Alternatively, you can contact the Pay and Work Rights helpline for confidential help and advice about the NMW (details below).

On 1 October 2009 the NWM was set at £5.80 for adult workers aged 22 and over. The development rate for workers aged 18–21 inclusive was set at £4.83 an hour. If you are 16 or 17 years old (above the compulsory school leaving age) the rate has been set at £3.57. This represents a 1.2 per cent increase on the previous year, which is the lowest rise since a statutory minimum wage was introduced in April 1999. However, modest though the increase is, the Government resisted calls from employers and the British Chambers of Commerce to peg the rate until there was significant improvement in the economy.

As a student employee, you will find that part-time wages vary considerably depending on the type of work that you do. As a general guide, the following positions and rates were advertised by university employment services in the Midlands in 2009:

- sales assistant in town centre clothes shop: £6.00 per hour;
- counter staff, out of town fish bar: £5.80 per hour;
- burger bar supervisor (city centre): £7.50 per hour;
- glass collector on university campus: £5.80 per hour;
- note-takers for students with hearing difficulties: £8.00 per lecture (untrained), £9.60 per lecture (trained);
- security staff for university entertainment: £25.00 per event;
- local football ground (hospitality): £8.75 per hour,
- waitress in town centre restaurant: £5.80 per hour plus equal share of tips;
- forecourt attendant: £5.80 per hour;
- student union bar staff: £5.80 per hour plus bonuses for weekend work;
- call centre sales staff: £5.80 plus bonuses.

Additional sources of financial support

If you have decided to study on a full-time basis, you are also eligible to apply for various types of student financial support. This could include the following:

- student loans;
- maintenance grants;
- university bursaries;
- Disabled Students' Allowances;

- grants for childcare and dependants;
- educational grants from charities or trusts;
- Access to Learning Funds (England);
- Hardship Funds (Scotland);
- Support Funds (Northern Ireland);
- Financial Contingency Funds (Wales);
- prizes won for academic excellence;
- scholarships;
- sponsorship;
- research awards;
- trade union funding (see Chapter 7).

More information about these sources of finances can be obtained from *The Essential Guide to Paying for University* (see below). If you intend to study on a part-time basis there are other grants and bursaries available; these are discussed in Chapter 25.

I worked as a note-taker while I was studying for my degree… I had to go on a three day training course, well, I didn't have to go on it, but if I did the training I got more money and I thought it would be useful for me anyway. The course was run by the university during the summer so I didn't miss any lectures or anything and it was easy to get to because I was in the city anyway. So I went on the course… I think there were about 30 of us, although a couple dropped out, I'm not sure why. I finished the course and then I worked as a note-taker for the first two years of my degree… I decided not to do it in the final year because I wanted to concentrate on my work, but it was really good for the first two years… They purposely made you go to different lectures from what you do, you know, a different subject because I think it might make you concentrate more… so I went to a whole lot of different lectures, which was quite interesting for me… You have to take notes about everything, including the way the lecturer says something, or if they make a joke and things because obviously a deaf person doesn't know that. I really enjoyed it and it helped me with money. I did go overdrawn in the end, you know, in the last year, but not half as bad as my mates. *Martina, 24, Sheffield Hallam University*

Eligibility criteria

Employers will specify their own eligibility criteria for positions, so contact them direct for more information. In general you will need to show enthusiasm, commitment, ability and reliability. For certain positions you will need to demonstrate that you have the required skills, competence and knowledge to undertake the type of work for which you are applying.

If you are hoping to obtain financial support for your studies, in most cases you will need to be from a low income family, have a disability and/or dependants, or have achieved high grades on entry. You may also be able to receive financial support if you excel at sports or music. You (and your parents, if relevant) will have to provide proof of your financial circumstances when you apply for financial support. For information about the specific eligibility criteria for the different types of grant and loan available for study at higher education level, visit the relevant student finance website (details below).

Application procedure

Application procedures will vary depending on the type of job. In most cases you will be required to complete an application form or produce a CV and attend an interview. Some employers may ask that you undertake a trial period before you are offered a permanent position. Visit your university employment service or careers service for advice and information about applying for jobs and increasing your chance of success. More information and advice can be obtained from www.prospects.ac.uk.

Applications for financial support for full-time students are made through the relevant student finance website (details below) or you can obtain further information from the student finance section of your local authority. Calculators are available on the student finance websites to help you work out how much money you could receive. This will help you decide whether you need to obtain a part-time and/or vacation job, and if so, how much you will need to earn to finance your studies.

Progression routes

Obtaining part-time and vacation work while you are studying will help you to pay for your course and help to alleviate money worries that could distract you from your studies. Since the introduction of variable tuition fees in 2006 it has been predicted that students will leave university with a debt of £15,000 – £18,000. If you are able to pay for your living costs and tuition fees while you are studying, you will be able to reduce your debt on graduation, or it may even be possible to graduate debt-free.

Future employers will be keen to see that you have had previous work experience and this may help you to secure a job when your studies have finished. This is of particular importance at this present time when we are experiencing increasing levels of graduate unemployment due to the recession. (A recent report by the Association of Graduate Recruiters suggests that, in 2009, there was an average of 48 applicants for each graduate post.) You will need to stand out from other graduates, and a good way to do this is to show that you have plenty of work experience in addition to the qualifications you have obtained.

Further information

Useful websites

www.nases.org.uk

The National Association of Student Employment Services (NASES) is the national representative body for practitioners from all types of student employment service. On the NASES website you can find an alphabetical list of student employment services in universities throughout the United Kingdom. The website contains information leaflets covering issues such as applying for jobs, income tax and national insurance.

www.direct.gov.uk

More information about your employment rights and the national minimum wage can be obtained from this website. Enter 'national minimum wage' into the search box to be directed to the relevant section of the website.

For more information about all aspects of financial support for students, visit the relevant student finance website:

England: www.studentfinanceengland.co.uk.
Wales: www.studentfinancewales.co.uk.
Northern Ireland: www.studentfinanceni.co.uk.
Scotland: www.saas.gov.uk.

Useful telephone numbers

Pay and Work Rights helpline: 0800 917 2368 (text phone for people with hearing difficulties: 0800 121 4042).

Further reading

For more information about all aspects of paying for your university education, see Dawson, C (2009) *The Essential Guide to Paying for University: Effective funding strategies for parents and students*, London: Kogan Page (£9.99).

27 Gap Years, Placements and Sponsorship

Gap years, work placements and sponsorship offer students the opportunity to earn and learn at higher education level, often paying for all or part of their course. If you are hoping to study at university, you may decide to spend some time in full-time employment saving enough money to pay for your studies, or you may decide to enrol on a course that has an element of work placement and/or attracts sponsorship that will help you to pay for part of your tuition and maintenance. Work placements could be in the vacations or for a whole year of your degree course. Sponsorship could be offered for part, or all, of your course.

This chapter describes the type of gap year, work placement and sponsorship schemes that are available, and includes information about the level of wages, the eligibility criteria, application procedures and progression routes, concluding with useful websites.

Type of scheme

Gap years

In the traditional meaning of the phrase, a gap year is taken to be a year away from full-time study between the completion of full-time further education (usually A levels, at school or at college) and before the start of full-time higher education. However, if you are an adult student you can also take advantage of this type of earning potential, perhaps taking a break between different types of higher education course, sometimes dipping in an out of full- or part-time education while you earn enough money to pay for the next part of your course. The Credit Accumulation and Transfer System (CATS) enables you to build up credits towards your final qualification over a period of time, once you can afford to continue your studies. Modules can be studied at different universities and even in different European countries and credits are accumulated until the final award is achieved (see Chapter 25 for more information about CATS).

Gap year working opportunities can be in the United Kingdom or overseas. There is a wide variety of opportunities available, but if you are hoping to raise enough money to pay for your university studies, you will need to consider those that pay a good wage, rather than the voluntary opportunities or those that require you to pay a registration fee. Also, it is possible to choose work with an employer for whom you could work full-time once you have completed your studies, or for an employer who will offer you further vacation work if your finances should run low.

The type of work that you do depends on a number of factors, including the opportunities available in the area that you live or wish to work, your existing skills, talents, likes and dislikes, your personal motivation, current vacancies, current salary levels and perhaps a little bit of luck. An advantage to taking a gap year is that you can pick and choose the type of work you apply for, rather than be constrained by having to work in an area related to your course of study.

Work placements

Work placements are offered as part of your undergraduate degree course and as such will be related directly to your studies. Although this constrains your choices in terms of the type of work that you can do, the advantages are that the work placement is very relevant to your course and therefore will help you to secure work in the future. Also, it should help you to maintain motivation levels in work and study if you have chosen the course because it is an area that is of interest to you. It also helps you to put into practice the theory that you learn, and it helps you to relate your work to your studies, perhaps providing useful research data for your final year dissertation (this is an extended project involving personal research on a topic of your choice).

Degree courses that offer work placements can be called 'sandwich courses', or they are described as four-year degree courses with a one-year work placement. This type of course tends to be more popular in subjects such as engineering, technology, management and languages, with some students using their work placement to work overseas. Alternatively, some students choose to study part-time with elements of work placement taking place at different times throughout the course. Others choose to study full-time and carry out their work placements during the vacations.

Company sponsorship

Some companies are willing to sponsor students through their studies by providing an agreed sum of money for one, two, three or four years of study. Contracts vary considerably. If a company offers a significant amount of money it will expect you to work for it for a certain number of years after completing your studies.

However, this type of sponsorship is now quite rare. Instead, companies tend to offer smaller sums, providing working opportunities through vacations and during sandwich years or placements. This type of sponsorship tends not to tie you into working for the company once you have graduated, although many students find that they are offered a job on successful completion of their course.

In general, companies are interested in vocational courses or those that provide the opportunity for work placement. The following subject areas receive the most sponsorship:

- civil, structural, electrical and mechanical engineering;
- physical sciences;
- information technology and computing;
- business management;
- financial management;
- banking;
- law;
- economics;
- medicine;
- dentistry.

If the subject area in which you are interested is not listed here, contact your course tutor or relevant companies direct to find out if there are sponsorship opportunities available.

Amount of money

Gap years

Salary levels vary enormously, depending on the type of work that you undertake. The best paid jobs tend to be those that require high-level qualifications, lengthy training and/or considerable talent. If you are a school leaver, you may not have the qualifications or training required to obtain this kind of job. However, it may be possible to convince an employer that you have the necessary talent (or potential), even if you do not have the required experience and qualifications.

Some employers are willing to look favourably on applications from gap year students, first because they can pay less than they would need to for a fully qualified employee, and secondly because they are employing you on a temporary basis and therefore do not need to assign you the same employment rights as someone on a permanent contract. You can use these points to your advantage when looking for suitable opportunities. Although you may be paid less than a fully qualified, permanent worker, you can still negotiate a decent salary that to you, if you are a school leaver, represents a considerable amount of money.

Work placements

Again, salary levels vary enormously depending on the type of work that you undertake. In most cases you should be offered a competitive wage that is comparable to that of other trainees. Contact individual employers, or speak to staff in the university placement unit, to find out what wages you can expect on your placement. You should note that if you are a student doing work experience as part of your higher or further education course you are not entitled to the national minimum wage (NMW) if the work experience does not last longer than a year. In practice, however, universities work closely with employers who provide work placements and make sure that employers provide valuable work experience and a decent wage for their students. For current levels of the NMW see Chapter 26.

Company sponsorship

The amount of money offered varies enormously and will depend on what you, and the company, want to get out of the agreement. Some students may receive a large sum that is enough to cover tuition fees and living expenses for three or four years. In some cases this may be up to £9,000 a year. If you receive this type of sponsorship, the company will need to make sure that you pay back what you have been given in terms of how long you work for that company after graduation. You will need to sign a contract in which you agree to its terms and conditions, so you must check that you are happy with the contract before you sign.

Other companies will give small amounts of money, maybe for specific projects, or for only one year of study. This could be any amount up to £3,000. In these circumstances you may not be tied into a long-term contract with the company.

Corus is one of the world's largest steel producers with operating facilities in the United Kingdom, the Netherlands, Germany, France and Belgium. The company offers work placements for students which can last from three months to a year and pays £14,500 per year (2009 levels). Opportunities are available in a variety of roles. Training is tailored to meet your individual needs and the needs of your placement role, and is mostly on the job. You will have regular meetings with your manager to assess your performance. As a placement student in the United Kingdom, if you successfully complete at least a three-month placement over the summer period you are eligible to apply for sponsorship from Corus. Currently this is worth £1,500 paid in three instalments of £500, one per academic term. Continued sponsorship throughout the academic year is dependent on you achieving at least a 2:1 average and good reports from your university tutor. To find out more about these placement opportunities and sponsorship deals, visit www.corusgroup.com.

Armed services sponsorship

Sponsorship is offered by all armed services at further and higher education level (see the case study below). For general information about the range of opportunities in the Army, you can telephone 08457 300 111. For information about joining the Army as an officer and for sponsorship opportunities, visit your local Army Careers Office or consult www.armyjobs.mod.uk. More information about sponsorship by the Royal Navy can be obtained from www.careers.royalnavy.mod.uk, or you can request specific information and advice by ringing the Recruitment Line on 08456 075 555. For more information about careers in the RAF and sponsorship deals visit www.rafcareers.com. If you wish to speak to a careers adviser you can telephone 0845 605 5555, or contact the Armed Forces Careers Liaison Officer via careers staff at your school or your local Connexions office.

Connor's always wanted to go into the Army because that's what his dad does. Connor's dad went to Welbeck (the Defence Sixth Form College, near Loughborough) but Connor wanted to go to university. So he went for sponsorship from the Army for his studies and he got it... They paid £6,000 for his degree course, which obviously didn't cover everything but it really helped. He had to agree to stay in service for at least three year after he'd finished at university but that wasn't a problem because he knows this is what he wants to do for a career. He had to attend an RMAS course (Royal Military Academy Sandhurst) for officer training and he also had to take part in training and exercises over the summer holidays when he was studying... I think he got paid for the training while he was studying but I'm not sure. Anyway he's now in the army following in his dad's footsteps. The money didn't make a difference because that's what he wanted to do anyway, although it helped him pay for university so that was a bonus really. *Laura, Connor's mum, Coventry*

Eligibility criteria

Eligibility criteria for gap year jobs, work placements and sponsorship vary, depending on the type of work that you want to undertake. In general you will need to demonstrate enthusiasm, commitment, reliability, team-working abilities, good communication skills and the ability to carry out the role efficiently and effectively. In most cases an employer will want to know that you are doing well on your course and that you are enthusiastic about your subject and the type of work that you will undertake. For larger amounts of sponsorship money you will have to sign a contract and agree to work for the organisation for a specified amount of time after graduation. If you break the agreement you may have to pay back some or all of the money you have received in sponsorship. Armed services sponsorship has strict eligibility criteria in terms of residency, nationality, health and fitness, height, age and sex (in some areas of service) so you will need to make sure that you meet these requirements if you are interested in armed services sponsorship.

Since some work placements are a compulsory component of your course, you will first of all need to be accepted on the degree course. To do this you will need to achieve the required number of UCAS tariff points. This is the system for allocating points to qualifications used for entry to higher education. It allows students to use a range of different qualifications to help secure a place on an undergraduate course. Visit www.ucas.ac.uk to find out how many points are awarded to different qualifications. Applications for a university place are made through UCAS (see below).

Application procedure

Gap years

In most cases applying for gap year work is similar to applying for any other job, apart from the fact that your potential employer will understand that you will only be working for a year before you begin, or return to, your studies. You will need to complete an application form or produce a CV and attend an interview or selection day.

Work placements

If you hope to study on a full-time sandwich course or another type of course with an element of work placement involved, you will apply in the usual way through UCAS; for more information, visit www.ucas.ac.uk. If you intend to study part-time, applications are made direct to your chosen university. Contact them for a part-time prospectus and application form. More information about part-time study at higher education level is provided in Chapter 25.

Most universities that offer sandwich courses or a compulsory work placement element on the course have a 'placement unit' or a 'placement tutor', able to work with students to make sure that they receive the most suitable placement. This saves you a lot of time-consuming research, and applications are much easier and less formal because most of the employers on the placement list already work with the university and have accepted placement students in the past. You may need to complete an application form and attend a selection interview, although this is not always the case.

If you intend to apply for work placement that is not part of your course, you will need to do so in the usual way by completing an application form and/or CV and attending an interview.

Sponsorship

Most companies will want to know that you have been offered a university place before they will consider sponsoring you. However, some companies work closely with specific universities so if you know that you want to follow this route, contact the company in which you are interested prior to making your UCAS application. That way you can make sure that your choice of university and course is suitable for the company.

Applying for sponsorship is similar to applying for a job, especially if you will be working for that company during the vacations or when you have completed your studies. You will need to show that you are keen to work for the company, you are committed to your studies and you will not break any contract that you have signed.

If you are interested in armed services sponsorship you will need to undergo a selection procedure that involves various tests. These tend to take place over two days and include aptitude tests, practical initiative tests, gym tests and interviews. More information about the selection procedures for each of the armed services can be obtained from the telephone numbers and websites given above.

Progression routes

Gap years, work placements and some types of sponsorship enable you to work full-time with an employer to gain experience and develop your skills. Future employers look favourably on this type of experience and your CV will stand out from other graduates who do not have it. Some students find that they are able to secure employment with their placement employers once they have successfully completed their studies. Indeed, the 'Everything you wanted to know' website points out that many companies take 60 per cent or more of their graduate intake each year from students who have been on sponsorship or placement programmes (details below). Others are able to convince their placement employers to sponsor them through a further year of postgraduate study.

If you have received a significant amount of sponsorship money for your studies you will have signed a contract stating that you will work for an agreed amount of time for the company. This means that you are guaranteed a job at the end of your studies, as long as the company remains in business and if you do not breach the terms of the contract. During times of recession and increasing graduate unemployment, this type of agreement can relieve many of the pressures associated with job-hunting and rising student debt.

Further information

Useful websites

www.work-experience.org

This is the website of the National Council for Work Experience (NCWE), an organisation that promotes, supports and develops work experience for the benefit of students, organisations and the economy. On this site you can read work placement case studies and access links to organisations offering work placements for students. You can also find out about the Quality Mark, which is an accreditation awarded by the NCWE to recognise employers that have reached the required standard of work experience provision.

www.prospects.ac.uk

Prospects is an organisation that provides careers advice for graduate students. On this website you can find information about a variety of organisations that offer year-long work placements, vacation placements, summer internships and trainee opportunities. You can also find information about producing CVs, attending job interviews and increasing your chances of success.

www.work-placement.co.uk

This site contains useful information about work placements, including details of the National Work Placement Exhibitions that take place in London and Birmingham. There is also some useful careers advice here.

www.itraineeship.com

This website seeks to match graduates with international employers. It provides detailed listings of a variety of international employers, work and placement opportunities, including short- and long-term contracts before, during and after your course.

www.targetjobs.co.uk

This website has a useful database that you can search for all kinds of jobs, including short-term jobs for work experience. You can search the database by sector, keyword and region.

www.topinternships.com

This website provides information on internships and placements for UK undergraduates. You can search the database by sector, discipline, date, location and keyword. You will need to register to view the results of your search.

www.everythingyouwantedtoknow.com

Visit the 'job/placement' section of this site to find out about sponsorship, placement and graduate opportunities.

www.scholarship-search.org.uk

Visit the 'sponsorship' section of the Hot Courses website to find out what opportunities are available. The listings provide details of the amount of sponsorship, duration, opening and closing dates for applications, number of awards and subject area. There is also a link to the relevant sponsor's website.

28 Entrepreneurs and Self-employment

An effective way to learn while you earn at higher education level is to become a student entrepreneur and/or set yourself up as self-employed. This can be done before your studies begin or while you are studying at university. Today, student entrepreneurship and self-employment are becoming increasingly popular activities with more organisations being set up, both within and outside of universities, to help students with their endeavours.

This chapter describes the type of schemes that are available, and includes information about the level of wages, the eligibility criteria, application procedures and progression routes, concluding with useful organisations and websites.

Type of scheme

If you wish to become a student entrepreneur or set yourself up as self-employed, there are three main ways of doing so: as a sole trader, in a partnership or as a limited company. Different rules and regulations apply to each method of trading and you should seek advice about the method most appropriate to your personal circumstances. Comprehensive information and advice about all aspects of setting up a business, including tailor-made, personal advice, can be obtained from your local Business Link. To obtain contact details and more information, visit www.businesslink.gov.uk.

If the business that you intend to set up in one of the three ways described below is related to your course in any way, you may find that it provides useful research data for projects and dissertations. Also, you may find that you can use what you have learnt on your course for the benefit of your business, and that you can use your business experiences to inform your course work.

A sole trader

Setting up as a sole trader is the simplest and most common way for students to run a business as there are less legal requirements involved. However, as a sole trader you are ultimately personally liable for any losses your business makes and creditors can pursue you for both business and personal assets.

If you decide to trade as a sole trader you will need to register with HM Revenue and Customs (HMRC) as self-employed. You will need to keep up-to-date books and records for tax purposes and submit an annual self-assessment tax return. More information and contact details of your local Inland Revenue Enquiry Centre can be obtained from www.hmrc.gov.uk.

I'm really not very good working for other people, never have been... don't know why, just my personality I guess. I spent loads of time thinking about what I could (do) to earn money and have money still coming in while I went off and did other things like travel and all that, you know, go to festivals and spend lots of time recovering without having to get up and go to work. So I thought of writing, which I've always enjoyed so I did one of those correspondence courses, you know, one that says you can make money from writing before you finish the course. And I did, which surprised me, but I did... So I became a writer, which I'm not saying was (not) a hard slog because it was. It took at least eight years to get there.... Then I thought I wanted to go and do a degree 'cos I finished school after A levels and I'd always wanted to do a degree and never done it. So that's when I thought I was really lucky 'cos I could carry on my writing while I studied. I was also a mature student so I wrote a piece for a local paper every month about how I was getting on for the whole three years... and with other things I could pay for my rent and for my food... yes I am classed as a sole trader, but that sounds a bit weird as a writer, but that is what I am... I do my tax forms each year, they're not too bad, although I did have a bit of problem about grants and things, you know, whether that counted, but I've found out it doesn't, so no, no problems at all and the writing certainly helped to pay for my course. Three more months to go, fingers crossed. *Susan, third year, Bournemouth University*

A partnership

If you intend to set up your company with someone else (perhaps another student or someone who can bring particular expertise to your business) you could think about setting up a partnership. With this type of agreement, you and your partner share the work, risks, costs and responsibilities of being in business. You are both self-employed and take a share of the profits. However, you are both also personally responsible for any debts that the business runs up.

Tax implications for a partnership are similar to becoming a sole trader: each partner will need to inform HMRC of their intention to become self-employed. Up-to-date accounts will need to be kept and both individuals, and the partnership, will need to submit an annual self-assessment tax return.

A limited company

There are two types of limited company. A private limited company is the most typical set-up for small businesses in the United Kingdom. It cannot offer shares to the public, but can have private shareholders. A public limited company, on the other hand, is permitted to sell shares to the public and raise funds in this way. Although legal requirements, rules, regulations and paperwork are more complex, your personal assets are safe in most cases. Establishing this type of company can be useful experience for business and management students and may provide interesting research data for university projects and your final-year dissertation. To set up a limited company, contact Companies House (www.companieshouse.gov.uk).

Limited companies will need to file annual accounts at Companies House and produce corporate tax returns each year. Tax issues for limited companies are much more complex, so if you are thinking of following this route you may need to obtain the services of an accountant (or an accountancy student, who may agree to help you as practical experience for his or her course). This person would be able to offer advice about discounts, savings and incentives that can help you to reduce your tax bill considerably, thus recuperating the fee for his or her services. To find an accountant in your area, visit the Institute of Chartered Accountants website (www.icaew.com) or contact the accountancy department at your university.

Amount of money

How much you earn will depend on a number of factors, including demand for your product or service, the amount of money you can charge, your overheads and your skills and competence (see case study below for an example of what you could earn). You should note that businesses fail because they are under-capitalised: starting a business costs money, and experiencing losses costs money, so you need to plan ahead to minimise potential losses. You also need to think about how you will cover running costs if you are unable to make enough sales or provide your service at certain times through the year. This could be when you are revising for, and taking, examinations. Will you be able to continue your business at this time? Will you be able to employ someone to work for you? Is it prudent to do so? How much will it cost? Enterprise offices have been established at many universities to help students with these issues, so you should seek further advice if in doubt (see further information, below).

Simon was studying computing at Kent University. He felt it would be quite lucrative to offer IT services to fellow students (and lecturers) while he was studying. However, he soon found out that students were not willing, or were unable, to pay for his services so he decided to advertise to local people in the Canterbury area instead. Although business was slow to pick up, he found that by his second year he was earning almost £7,000 by mending and building computers for people in the local area. As he was an independent student on a low income he was also able to receive a full grant, and a university bursary, which meant that he received around £11,000 from grants, bursaries and earned income in his second year. This amount was reduced slightly in his third year because he was revising for exams and completing his extended project and, therefore, could not spend so much time mending computers. However, through earning in this way Simon did not have to take out a student loan and was able to graduate debt-free. He graduated two years ago and has established an IT business, employing four people.

Tax

If you intend to set up in business you need to be aware of the tax issues as these may reduce the amount that you earn. The type of tax and how much you will have to pay depend on your answers to the following questions:

- Are you setting up in business as a self-employed individual, or as a company/limited liability partnership (see above)?
- Will anyone be working for you as an employee?
- How much turnover do you expect to have in your first year of business, and how much profit do you expect to make?

Depending on your answers to these questions, you may need to pay the following taxes:

- *Income tax.* You have a personal tax-free allowance of £6,475 (2009/10 figures); you will have to pay income tax on any earnings above this amount.
- *Corporation tax.* Companies pay this tax on profits to HMRC.
- *Value Added Tax (VAT).* If your taxable turnover hits £64,000 a year (or you expect it to), you must register for VAT.
- *Capital Gains Tax (CGT).* Individuals pay this tax if they make a certain amount of profit (gain) when they sell (dispose of) an asset.
- *Stamp duty.* This is collected on the purchase of property, stocks or shares, or when a long or high-value lease is signed.
- *Importing and exporting tax.* If you import goods from outside the European Union, you may have to pay taxes on them.
- *Pay As You Earn (PAYE).* If you employ other people you will be responsible for calculating and paying this tax and National Insurance Contributions.

National Insurance Contributions

If you are self-employed and over the age of 16 you pay Class 2 National Insurance Contributions (NICs) at a flat-rate weekly amount of £2.40 (2009/10 figures). It is possible to apply for the Small Earnings Exception (SEE) if you know that you will earn below £5,075 in the tax year, so you would not need to pay Class 2 contributions. You also pay Class 4 NICs as a percentage of your taxable profits: you pay 8 per cent on annual taxable profits between £5,715 and £43,875 and 1 per cent on any taxable profit over that amount (2009/10 figures).

Eligibility criteria

There are no eligibility criteria for becoming a student entrepreneur or self-employed. All you need is a good, workable idea; the enthusiasm, commitment and time; the required skills, knowledge, expertise or the willingness and ability to acquire them; the necessary finances or the ability to raise them.

Some universities have regulations in place to limit the number of hours a week that students spend in paid employment, so you will need to check that these are not breached. However, as a self-employed person you may not have set working hours, nor are the hours that you work regularly recorded. Nevertheless, you will need to make sure that you are able to balance your work and study commitments, and that neither has a detrimental impact on the other.

Application procedure

No application is required, apart from the usual UCAS application for your degree course. If you are hoping to raise finances from an external backer, you may need to complete a detailed application form and produce a profit/loss plan and a cash flow forecast. A profit/loss plan is a careful assessment of what you expect to happen with the income and expenditure of your business and will help you to determine whether your project is feasible. A cash flow forecast will show you how much money you need to set up and run your business. The university enterprise office should be able to help you with this, or you can contact your local Business Link (details above).

Progression routes

Your business may do so well that you are able to continue and grow once you have completed your studies, and some students find that their business is so successful that they leave university debt-free (see case study above). Even if you decide not to continue with your business, employers will look favourably on the expertise that you have developed as a result of your entrepreneurship. This will help you to stand out from other graduates and secure a better, more fulfilling and well-paid job after your studies.

The skills that you could learn from your entrepreneurship are many and could include financial management, communication skills, teamwork, organisational skills, management and leadership, IT skills, social skills, delegation skills and the ability to develop contacts, win contracts and network. All of these will help you to secure future employment and will be useful for life in general.

Further information

Useful organisations

Entrepreneur offices

Many universities now have a student entrepreneur office and staff within this office will be able to offer advice and guidance on the help that is available. Through working closely with staff you will be able to obtain free professional advice, network with other student entrepreneurs and find out about free training courses, conferences and entrepreneurial competitions, all of which will help you to build your business.

Entrepreneur societies

Many universities have an Entrepreneur Society that enables you to meet with like-minded students to discuss inspirational ideas, meet possible partners and obtain support and advice. Contact your university students' union to find out whether such a society exists. If it does not, you could think about setting one up. Advice and guidance on doing so can be obtained from your students' union. Two examples of these societies can be viewed at www.oxfordentrepreneurs.co.uk and www.fishontoast.com.

HM Revenue and Customs Advice Teams

If you are thinking of working for yourself or have just started, you can attend a free workshop with the HMRC Advice Team. It can provide practical advice on tax issues, VAT registration, record-keeping, filling in and filing your tax return and employing people. For more information and to book a place in a workshop, visit www.hmrc.gov.uk/startingup. Alternatively, for further information about workshops and presentations you can phone 0845 603 2691.

Useful websites

www.speedproject.ac.uk

Student Placements for Entrepreneurs in Education (SPEED) is a project led by Wolverhampton University with many other universities taking part. The aim of the project is to provide students with the skills and knowledge they need to start up their own businesses. Visit the site for more information about the project.

http://royalsociety.org/enterprisefund

On this site you can find out more information about Royal Society funding to help entrepreneurs to commercialise their ideas. It is available to help UK scientists and engineers (including students) to turn their inventions into businesses.

www.princes-trust.org.uk

If you are aged between 18 and 30 and have a business idea, the Prince's Trust may be able to help with advice and funding. This website contains information about the type of help and support that may be available.

29 Professional Training and Loans

In some professions you can work as a trainee and study towards a higher education qualification while receiving a wage. For other professions it is possible to receive a loan to help you to pay for your tuition fees and maintenance while you study on a full-time basis. If you want to work towards an undergraduate or postgraduate qualification in a profession such as teaching, social work, healthcare, management or law, these schemes may be of interest to you.

This chapter describes schemes that are available for professional training and study at undergraduate and postgraduate level, and provides information about the amount of money, the eligibility criteria, application procedures and progression routes, concluding with useful organisations, useful websites and contact numbers.

Type of scheme

There is a variety of professions that enable you to study for a higher education qualification while you are working and receiving a wage. There are different levels of qualification for which you can study, and your eligibility to enter at each level will depend on your previous qualifications and work experience.

A Framework for Higher Education Qualifications (FHEQ) has been designed by the higher education sector, and contains descriptions of all the main higher education qualifications. It applies to degrees, diplomas, certificates and other academic awards granted by a university or higher education college (apart from honorary degrees and higher doctorates), and is relevant to England, Wales and Northern Ireland. In Scotland the Scottish Credit and Qualifications Framework (SCQF) is the equivalent (www.scqf.org.uk). For more information about the framework, and to find out more about higher education qualifications in general, visit the Quality Assurance Agency for Higher Education website (details below). This will help you to work out whether the level of qualification offered through your professional training will be suitable for your needs. If you are from overseas, you can find out how your professional qualifications compare with UK qualifications by visiting www.naric.org.uk.

Examples of some of the professions that enable you to learn while you earn are provided below. If you are interested in another type of profession that is not discussed below, contact the relevant professional association for more information about whether employment-based learning, or other types of funding such as bursaries and grants, are available for your studies.

Teacher training

There are three types of employment-based training that enable you to train and qualify as a teacher while working in a school:

1. The Graduate Teacher Programme enables you to undertake on-the-job training, earn a salary and work towards qualified teacher status (QTS), while employed by a school. It is useful for mature people who wish to change careers but still want to earn a wage while they are learning. The programme usually takes one school year to complete. More information about this scheme can be obtained from the Training and Development Agency for Schools (TDA) (details below).
2. The Registered Teacher Programme enables non-graduates to work towards QTS through a mix of work-based teacher training and academic study. The programme usually takes two years to complete. More information about this scheme can be obtained from the TDA (details below).
3. Teach First is an initiative that has been set up to encourage top graduates to work in challenging secondary schools, working towards QTS and undertaking leadership training and work experience with leading employers. Teach First takes two years to complete. For more information about this scheme, visit http://graduates.teachfirst.org.uk.

Healthcare

There is a wide variety of opportunities in healthcare and allied health professions. For some professions you will be able to learn on the job, receiving a trainee wage and studying towards your qualification on a part-time basis. For other professions you will be required to study full-time at university and there are bursaries available to help you to pay for your studies. The courses involve a mix of theoretical and practical studies, and contain a large amount of practical work experience, for which you are paid a placement allowance on top of your bursary. For a detailed breakdown of the type of opportunities that are available, visit www.nhscareers.nhs.uk.

Social work

If you are interested in social work there are employment-based courses available at degree level that enable you to work and receive a wage while you study on a part-time basis. If you prefer, you can study full-time and there are bursaries available for your studies, in addition to a practice learning opportunity (work placement) allowance. If you choose the employment-based option you will not be eligible to receive a social work bursary. More information about all the options available to you can be obtained from the relevant Care Council (details below).

Association of MBAs Loan Scheme

This scheme provides a loan for full- and part-time students who wish to study for a Master of Business Administration (MBA) qualification. The Association of MBAs operates the scheme, which is financed by the NatWest Bank. For more information visit http://graduate.mbaworld.com or phone NatWest on 0800 015 1166.

Professional loan schemes

If you are interested in studying for a profession, such as law or medicine, there are other loans available. For example, NatWest offers the Professional Trainee Loan Scheme and the College of Law Loan Scheme. Lloyds TSB and the Royal Bank of Scotland also run loan schemes specifically for law students. For more information about these schemes, eligibility criteria and application procedures, visit the relevant bank website (details below) or contact your local branch. It is also possible to apply for a Career Development Loan for professional studies (see Chapter 20).

Amount of money

Teacher training

For the employment-based teacher training schemes your school will pay you an unqualified or qualified teacher's salary (anywhere from £15,113 depending on your responsibilities, experience and location). There may be additional grants available, depending on what you intend to teach and the type of scheme.

Healthcare

If you intend to take part in employment-based learning in the healthcare sector you will be paid the relevant trainee or unqualified wage. If you are hoping to enrol on a healthcare course and undertake work experience, the amount of money available depends on a number of factors. These include the type of course, your household income, your childcare/dependant needs, the length of your work placement and the location in which you are studying and working. A calculator is available at www.nhsstudent-grants.co.uk to help you to work out how much money you could receive.

Social work

The amount of money available for social work courses and work placements depends on whether you are studying full- or part-time, where you are studying and working, and the length of time of your placement. For example, if you are studying on a full-time course that is subject to variable tuition fees, the maximum grant available is £4,975 in London and £4,575 elsewhere (2009 figures). This includes a fixed contribution of £575 towards placement travel expenses. If you are on an employment-based course you will continue to receive your usual wage while you are studying and will not be eligible to apply for the grant.

The MBA Loan Scheme

The MBA Loan Scheme will provide a loan that is worth up to two-thirds of your gross annual pre-course salary, plus tuition fees and expenses, less any income from sponsors and grants for full-time students. Part-time students can borrow enough to cover tuition fees and study equipment. You can borrow up to £10,000 if you are a distance learner. Students do not have to make any repayments while they are studying.

Professional loans

The Professional Trainee Loan Scheme from NatWest Bank enables you to borrow up to £20,000 (£25,000, if you are studying full-time for the Graduate Diploma in Law (GDL), Legal Practice Course (LPC) or Bar Vocational Course (BVC)). You can draw the loan in one lump sum or instalments and you do not have to make any repayments for at least six months after you finish your course. You have up to 10 years to repay your loan.

The Lloyds TSB Professional Studies Loan is available in law and is up to £10,000 or two-thirds of your previous salary if in employment. Repayment is over a period of five years maximum, beginning six months after you complete your course. The Royal Bank of Scotland Law Student Loan Scheme offers up to £15,000 with a repayment period of seven years.

Eligibility criteria

Teacher training

To be eligible for employment-based teacher training schemes, you must meet the following qualification requirements:

- The Graduate Teacher Programme will require qualifications at least equivalent to a UK bachelors degree and GCSE grade C or above in mathematics and English. If you intend to teach primary or Key Stage 2/3 (ages 7–14), you must also have achieved a standard equivalent to a grade C in a GCSE science subject.
- The Registered Teacher Programme will require GCSE grade C or above in mathematics and English. If you intend to teach primary or

Key Stage 2/3 (ages 7–14), you must also have achieved a standard equivalent to a grade C in a GCSE science subject. You will also need to have completed the equivalent of two years of higher education. This is the equivalent of 240 Credit and Accumulation and Transfer Scheme (CATS) points, and can include diplomas and certificates, for example. For more information about CATS, see Chapter 25.

- Teach First will require the following:
    - a 2.1 degree or above;
    - over 300 UCAS points (or equivalent);
    - a grade C (or equivalent) in GCSE maths and English;
    - the flexibility to work anywhere within East Midlands, London, North West, West Midlands and Yorkshire;
    - high levels of competence in areas such as leadership, teamwork, resilience and critical thinking.

Healthcare

To be eligible for healthcare courses and employment-based learning you will need to meet the qualification requirements specified for each profession, listed at www.nhscareers.nhs.uk. If you are hoping to obtain a bursary while you are studying, there are residency conditions attached; these can be viewed at www.nhsstudentgrants.co.uk. You will also need to check that you are studying on a qualifying course. Your course tutor should be able to advise you on this.

Social work

For social work bursaries you will need to be studying on a qualifying course and meet the residency requirements. These are available at www.nhsstudentgrants.co.uk (this organisation administers both healthcare and social work bursaries). If you are interested in employment-based learning, more information about eligibility can be obtained from the relevant Care Council (details below).

The MBA Loan Scheme

To qualify for an MBA Loan you must meet the following conditions:

- You must be over 18 and usually not over 40 years old at the time of application.
- You must be a permanent UK passport holder or possess indefinite leave to remain within the United Kingdom (three years' minimum residency prior to commencement of study).
- You must have a place on an MBA programme accredited by the Association of MBAs (the scheme is also available to individuals who have a place on selected leading MBA programmes outside the United Kingdom).
- You must have at least five years' practical work experience within industry or commerce or, if you are a graduate, you must have at least three years' work experience.
- You are expected to make a contribution from your own funds equal to 20 per cent of the total course fees.

Professional loans

To be eligible to apply for a loan through the Professional Trainee Loan Scheme at NatWest Bank you must be studying full-time for a professional qualification to become one of the following:

- barrister;
- chiropodist or podiatrist;
- chiropractor;
- dentist;
- doctor;
- optician;
- osteopath;
- pharmacist;
- physiotherapist;
- solicitor;
- veterinary surgeon.

You do not have to be an existing customer of NatWest to apply for this loan. However, Lloyds TSB and the Royal Bank of Scotland schemes require you to be an existing customer, or you can transfer your account to the bank before applying. For more information about eligibility criteria, contact the relevant bank (details below).

Application procedure

More information about applying for employment-based teacher training can be obtained from the TDA website (details below). For specific information about applying to the Teach First scheme, visit http://graduates. teachfirst.org.uk.

Application forms for bursaries for healthcare and social work courses and work placement allowances can be downloaded from www.nhsstudentgrants.co.uk.

To download an application form for the MBA Loan Scheme, visit http:// graduate.mbaworld.com or you can obtain a form by telephoning NatWest on 0800 015 1166. Visit the relevant bank website to find out about application procedures for other types of professional loan (details below).

Progression routes

All these schemes are designed to help you to gain qualifications while you are working within your professional role or through a large amount of work placement during your full-time studies. This will enable you to gain new knowledge and skills that you can apply to your employment. You can also choose to carry out practical, hands-on research for your academic studies within your working environment. Gaining both work experience and qualifications will enable you to work more effectively and efficiently, and it will open up more career choices and possibilities in the future. In most cases you will receive a higher wage if you have the relevant professional qualification.

Further information

Useful organisations

For enquiries concerning NHS and social work financial support in England, contact:

NHS Student Grants Unit
Hesketh House, 200–220 Broadway, Fleetwood, Lancashire FY7 8SS
Tel: (0845) 358 6655; Fax: (01253) 774490; e-mail: bursary@nhspa.gov.uk;
website: www.nhsstudentgrants.co.uk

For enquiries concerning NHS financial support in Wales contact:

The NHS Wales Student Awards Unit
3rd Floor, 14 Cathedral Road, Cardiff CF11 9LJ
Tel: (029) 2019 6167 (bursary enquiries); Tel: (029) 2019 6168 (childcare enquiries); e-mail: use contact form on website: www.nliah.com

For enquiries concerning NHS financial support in Scotland contact:

The Student Awards Agency for Scotland
3 Redheughs Rigg, South Gyle, Edinburgh EH12 9HH
Tel: (0845) 111 1711; Fax: (0131) 244 5887; e-mail: use contact form on website: www.saas.gov.uk

For enquiries concerning NHS financial support in Northern Ireland contact:

Nursing Board NI
Central Services Agency, Bursary Administration Unit, 2 Franklin Street, Belfast BT2 8 DQ
Tel: (028) 9055 3661; e-mail: use contact form on website: www.centralservicesagency.com

If you live in Wales contact the Care Council for Wales for more information about funding for social work:

Care Council for Wales
Student Funding Team, 7th Floor, South Gate House, Wood Street, Cardiff CF10 1EW
Tel: (0845) 070 0249; e-mail: studentfunding@ccwales.org.uk; website: www.ccwales.org.uk

If you live in Scotland contact the Scottish Social Services Council for more information about social work:

Social Services Council
Compass House, 11 Riverside Drive, Dundee DD1 4NY
Tel: (0845) 60 30 891; e-mail: enquiries@sssc.uk.com; website: www.sssc.uk.com

If you live in Northern Ireland contact the Northern Ireland Social Care Council for more information about social work:

Northern Ireland Social Care Council (NISCC)
7th Floor, Millennium House, 19–25 Great Victoria Street, Belfast BT2 7AQ
Tel: (028) 9041 7600; Fax: (028) 9041 7601;
e-mail: info@nisocialcarecouncil.org.uk; website: www.niscc.info

Useful websites

www.qaa.ac.uk
This is the website of the Quality Assurance Agency for Higher Education. On this site you can find out more information about higher education qualifications and the FHEQ, which applies to England, Wales and Northern Ireland.

www.tda.gov.uk
This is the website of the Training and Development Agency for Schools. On this site you can find out more information about employment-based training for schools and contact details of your local provider. You can register to receive information and advice about funding and other financial aspects of becoming a teacher, as well as regular news and updates about teaching and teacher training.

www.mbaworld.com
This is the website of the Association of MBAs. On this site you can find out more information about studying for an MBA and information about applying for a loan to help you to pay for your studies.

To find out more about professional loan schemes, visit the following bank websites:

NatWest: www.natwest.com
Lloyds TSB: www.lloydstsb.com
Royal Bank of Scotland: www.rbs.co.uk

Useful telephone numbers

Teaching information line: 0845 6000 991 (for English speakers), 0845 6000 992 (for Welsh speakers).
The Health Learning and Skills Advice Line: 08000 150 850.
More information about the NatWest MBA Loan can be obtained from 0800 015 1166.

Part Four

Learning and Earning as a Jobseeker

30 Entry to Employment (England)

Entry to Employment (e2e) is a scheme that is available for people aged 16 to 18 who live in England. Although it has been described as a 'pre-apprenticeship' scheme, it is in fact available to help young people obtain the skills that they need to progress on to an Apprenticeship, further learning or employment. On this scheme you will work closely with a personal tutor who will devise an education and training programme that meets your needs, so e2e programmes can vary considerably.

This chapter describes the e2e programme and provides information about the level of wages, the eligibility criteria, application procedures and progression routes, concluding with useful websites and contact numbers.

Type of scheme

This scheme provides the opportunity to undertake learning in three inter-dependent core areas:

1. basic and key skills;
2. vocational development;
3. personal and social development.

As the programme is based on the needs of the individual (depending on your learning capacity, aspirations, needs and progression choices) the number of hours attended each week and the duration of the programme can vary. As a general guide, it is usual for attendance to be for 16 to 30 hours a week for at least 10 weeks in duration. However, you can join e2e any time you choose and you can stay for as many weeks as you wish so that you can make the most of the opportunities available. It is also possible to work part-time alongside your e2e training. Through taking part in this programme you will improve your skills in literacy, numeracy and information technology, in addition to improving your personal confidence.

Learning can take place in a variety of indoor and outdoor settings, using a range of different learning methods such as one-to-one coaching, group discussions, online learning and various work placements. Examples of the types of course that you could take as part of your individual programme include the following:

- e2e Retail;
- e2e for Moderate Learning Difficulties;
- e2e Business Administration and Customer Service;
- e2e Travel and Tourism Certificate;
- e2e IT Certificate;
- e2e Fitness, Health and Lifestyle Certificate;
- e2e Construction Certificate;
- e2e Carpentry and Joinery Certificate;
- e2e Motor Vehicle Mechanics Certificate;
- e2e Body Repair and Refinishing Certificate;
- e2e Administration Certificate;
- e2e Painting and Decorating;
- e2e Literacy Certificate;
- e2e Numeracy Certificate;
- e2e Food Hygiene Certificate;
- e2e First Aid Certificate;
- e2e Dental Nursing;
- e2e Health and Social Care;
- e2e Childcare;
- e2e Catering.

Amount of money

Learners on an e2e programme can apply for an Education Maintenance Allowance (EMA). Since 30 June 2008 all eligible learners taking an e2e programme that is funded by the Learning and Skills Council (LSC) are entitled to the maximum EMA of £30 a week regardless of their household income. For more information about the LSC visit www.lsc.gov.uk.

For more information about the EMA visit http://ema.direct.gov.uk and see Chapter 12 of this book.

In addition to your EMA payment you will also be able to claim back daily travel expenses to and from your e2e training centre. If you have children you can apply for a Care to Learn grant that covers the costs of registered childcare while you attend e2e (see Chapter 23 for more information about this scheme).

Eligibility criteria

To be eligible for this programme you must live in England, be aged 16–18 and not currently employed on a full-time basis or participating in any form of post-16 learning. It may be possible for older people to take part in the programme, although this will be assessed on an individual basis.

Most people receive a referral to the scheme from a Connexions adviser or from social services. Careers advice offered during years 10 and 11 (when you are aged 14–16) at school may have identified the e2e programme as being suitable for your needs.

Application procedure

To find out more about this scheme contact your personal adviser at your local Connexions centre. To find your local centre visit www.connexions-direct.com or look in your local telephone directory. Alternatively, you can use one of the telephone numbers listed below to contact a Connexions Direct adviser who will be able to offer further information about the e2e programme. If they feel that the scheme would be of benefit to you, the adviser will be able to make a referral on your behalf. It is possible for you also to be referred to the scheme by social services or work-based learning providers.

To find out more about the e2e providers available in your area you can visit http://careersadvice-findacourse1.direct.gov.uk where you can search for all kinds of courses close to your home. Enter 'Entry to Employment' into the 'subject keywords' box and you will be able to find out more information about all the e2e learning providers locally. If you click on the provider in which you are interested you can find out more information about its e2e programme, including a course description, information on how long the course lasts and contact details.

Progression routes

Through attending this programme you will be able to improve your skills and increase your personal confidence, which should enable you to progress to an Apprenticeship, further learning or help you to find a job. For more information about Apprenticeships in England, see Chapter 1. For more information about learning and earning opportunities at further education level, see Part II of this book.

Further information

Useful websites

www.connexions-direct.com
Connexions is an organisation that provides information, advice and guidance to young people. On this website you can obtain more information about the e2e programme and contact a personal adviser for more information about the scheme and to find out whether it would be suitable for your needs.

http://e2e.lsc.gov.uk/documents
This website contains a number of documents about the e2e scheme that you may find useful. They include a *Simple Fact Sheet on Entry to Employment* and the *Framework for Entry to Employment Programmes*.

Useful telephone numbers

A Connexions Direct adviser can be contacted on 080 8001 3219. If you prefer to text you can do so on 07766 413 219. If you have hearing difficulties you can textphone on 08000 968 336.

31 Skill Build (Wales)

Skill Build is a programme available primarily for people aged 16–17 living in Wales who wish to develop their skills, improve their qualifications and find work. However, it can also be available for unemployed people of any age living in Wales. The scheme is funded by the Welsh Assembly Government and supported by the European Social Fund. The programme offers people the chance to start their career through a combination of learning options and work experience. It is ideal if you are unfocused, lack the confidence in your own ability or have been out of employment for any length of time.

This chapter describes the Skill Build programme and provides information about the level of wages, the eligibility criteria, application procedures and progression routes, concluding with useful websites and contact numbers.

Type of scheme

Skill Build enables you to try out a range of different work opportunities through work placements, 'taster' placements and short courses. Training providers work closely with local businesses to make sure that you can gain valuable work experience and improve your skills. You also receive help in preparing and searching for jobs. The scheme typically lasts for around 13 weeks, during which time you may be able to work towards an NVQ Level 1 (for more information about NVQs see Chapter 21). You will also work towards developing your key skills, in particular those that will help you to find work. These include:

- literacy;
- numeracy;
- information technology;

- working with others;
- problem solving;
- communication.

You are assigned a personal trainer/mentor who will work with you to develop your own Individual Learning Plan (ILP). This plan will include information about the training you are to undertake, the qualifications you already have, the qualifications required within your Skill Build framework and any other additional qualifications that you may be working towards. The plan will also contain information about how long your training will last and it will be reviewed on a regular basis during discussions with your trainer/mentor.

Once you have completed your Skill Build programme, it is possible to move onto Skill Build Plus, which enables you to take your training further and study for qualifications at a higher level. This part of the programme can take up to a year to complete. The type of areas that you could work within for both programmes include the following:

- animal care;
- construction;
- automotive engineering;
- administration and IT;
- retailing and customer service;
- hair and beauty;
- hospitality and catering;
- child care and elderly care.

Amount of money

If you are eligible and you are aged 16–18 you will be paid a training allowance of at least £50 a week (2009 figure). This amount will be paid for the duration of the Careers Wales agreement even if you are aged over 18 when you finish the programme (agreement to take part in Skill Build must be reached with your local Careers Wales office: see below). If you are aged 18 or over you will receive learning allowances payable by Jobcentre Plus. This will be an amount equivalent to the Jobseekers Allowance and/or Income Support plus a learning premium paid to undertake learning.

It may be possible to receive additional help with travel expenses to and from work placements. Also, if you have children, you may be able to receive help towards paying for registered childcare (see Chapter 23 for information about the childcare schemes that are available). Some trainees on the programme may be able to receive a clothing grant to help you to buy suitable clothes for interviews.

Eligibility criteria

Eligibility for this programme is determined by your local Careers Wales or Jobcentre Plus offices, so contact your local office direct to find out whether you qualify for the programme. In general, you will need to have recently completed your compulsory schooling and/or be unemployed, although it is possible to take part on the Skill Build Plus programme even if you are employed. Although this programme is primarily for people under the age of 18, it is possible for unemployed adults above this age to benefit from this scheme. If you are over the age of 18 and you are unemployed, contact Careers Wales or your local Jobcentre Plus to find out whether you could benefit from Skill Build and are eligible for the scheme.

Application procedure

Contact your local Careers Wales centre which will be able to offer advice about whether this scheme is suitable for you. If the adviser thinks that the scheme is suitable, he or she will refer you onto the programme and you will be assigned a personal trainer/mentor. He or she will also be able to provide details of local colleges and/or training providers that take part in the scheme. Depending on the type of course, you may be required to fill in an application form and/or attend an interview.

If you are an unemployed adult you can discuss the scheme with your personal adviser at your local Jobcentre Plus. He or she will be able to offer advice about whether the scheme is suitable for your needs or whether another scheme, such as New Deal, might be better (see Chapter 37). If he or she thinks that the scheme is suitable, you will be referred onto the programme and assigned a personal trainer/mentor.

Progression routes

The skills and qualifications that you gain through this programme can lead to a Foundation Modern Apprenticeship, Modern Apprenticeship or other employment opportunities. For more information about the Apprenticeship scheme in Wales, see Chapter 3. If you have been unemployed for some time, taking part in this scheme could help you to secure a job.

If you progress well you may be given the opportunity to work towards higher level NVQs and City & Guilds qualifications as part of the Skill Build Plus programme. Alternatively, you may choose to continue your learning at a further education college, perhaps in a vocational subject related to the type of work experience that you have undertaken. For more information about the learning and earning opportunities available in the further education sector, see Part II of this book.

Further information

Useful websites

www.careerswales.com
Careers Wales is funded by the Welsh Assembly Government and is available to give free careers information, advice and guidance to people of all ages in Wales. You can find out more information about Skill Build on this site, and the contact details of your local careers centre. The service is available in English and Welsh.

www.rathboneuk.org
Rathbone is a 'UK-wide voluntary youth sector organisation providing opportunities for young people to transform their life-circumstances by re-engaging with learning, discovering their ability to succeed and achieving progression to further education, training and employment'. Rathbone is one of the providers of the Skill Build programme in South and Mid Wales. It is also one of the providers of the e2e programme in England (see Chapter 30) and the Get Ready for Work programme in Scotland (see Chapter 32). Visit the website for more information about Rathbone and to read case studies about people who have taken part in the Skill Build programme.

www.acttraining.org.uk

Associated Community Training (ACT) was established in 1988 and is now one of the Welsh Assembly Government's leading skills training providers in Wales. ACT operates the Skill Build programme in various centres throughout south Wales. More information about the various programmes that are offered can be obtained from this website.

Useful telephone numbers

Learning and Careers Advice in Wales: 0800 100 900.

32 Get Ready for Work (Scotland)

Get Ready for Work is a national training programme in Scotland for young people to help them to move into a job, further education or training. It is funded by Skills Development Scotland and provides personal development, vocational, life and core skills for trainees who may find it difficult to obtain work without additional help. If you are aged 16–19 and you do not have a job or you are not already taking part in any education or training, this scheme may be of interest to you.

This chapter describes the Get Ready for Work scheme and provides information about the amount of money, the eligibility criteria, application procedures and progression routes, concluding with useful websites and contact numbers.

Type of scheme

The aim of the programme is to help you to move into employment, either directly straight into work, or indirectly through training and education programmes. Through this scheme you work with a Careers Scotland Personal Adviser to draw up an Individual Training Plan that is tailored to your needs and circumstances. Your personal adviser will help identify your individual needs and give you the skills and confidence you need to achieve your goals. This means that all Get Ready for Work plans differ, according to the needs of the individual. Help and advice that you could receive covers the following topics:

- interview techniques;
- producing a CV;
- completing application forms;
- improving your maths skills;

- improving your writing skills;
- enhancing your IT skills;
- managing your money;
- improving health and fitness;
- improving your teamworking skills;
- building up your self-confidence.

As part of the scheme you will have the opportunity to try different kinds of work through work tasters and placements, which will help you to find out what type of career interests you. Also, you may be able to work towards certain types of qualification that will improve your chances of securing a job in the future. These include nationally recognised qualifications in the following areas:

- customer care;
- first aid;
- information technology;
- retail and sales;
- food hygiene;
- hairdressing;
- sport and fitness.

A report called *Jobs for Youth: United Kingdom* published by the Organization for Economic Cooperation and Development in July 2009 reports that youth unemployment in the United Kingdom has risen from 11 to 14 per cent since 2002. Only 45 per cent of low-skilled youths have found jobs a year after leaving school. However, if young people achieve five good GCSEs, 67 per cent will have a job a year after they leave school. The report states that there is a 'high risk of poor labour market outcomes and social exclusion' for youngsters who leave school without qualifications. This is because changes in the economy means that there are more opportunities being created in the high-skills sector, while unskilled jobs are in decline. This report shows that you stand a better chance of obtaining work after leaving school if you are able to develop your skills further and obtain qualifications relevant to the work that you hope to do.

Amount of money

You will be paid a training allowance of at least £55 per week if you take part in the scheme on a full-time basis. All your training is free and you may be able to receive help with your travel expenses.

Eligibility criteria

To qualify for this scheme you must meet the following criteria:

● you must live in Scotland;
● you must be aged between 16 and 19;
● you must not be at school, college, employed or in training.

Application procedure

If you are interested in this scheme you should contact Careers Scotland on 0845 8502 502. An adviser will discuss your options and make sure that this scheme is suitable for your needs and circumstances. If it is deemed suitable you will work with a personal adviser to develop your training plan. You will then be placed with a learning/training provider (such as a local college or private training provider) that will deliver your individually tailored programme and ensure that your personal and vocational needs are met. You do not need to complete an application form or attend a selection interview to take part in this scheme. Also, most training providers work closely with local employers that will be able to offer you work experience, again without the need to complete an application form or attend an interview.

Progression routes

This scheme has been designed to help you to find work. Your personal adviser will work with you on the scheme to help you to achieve your goals, so that through additional education, training and/or work placements, you are equipped with the skills and confidence required to apply for, and secure, a job. Some people find that they would like to move onto an Apprenticeship after having completed their Get Ready for Work programme. More information about the Apprenticeship scheme in Scotland is provided in Chapter 2.

You may find that you enjoy your education and training and that you wish to take this further, perhaps by enrolling on a course at a further education college. Your personal adviser will be able to help you with decisions about further education and training. More information about the learning and earning schemes that are available in the further education sector is in Part II of this book.

Further information

Useful websites

www.careers-scotland.org.uk
You can find more information about the Get Ready for Work scheme on this website. You can also find out about other schemes that may be of interest to you, such as Skillseekers, Apprenticeships and the Training for Work scheme. This site contains useful information that will help you to create a CV, apply for jobs and succeed at job interviews. You can also download a series of 'Step to Success' leaflets from this site and use the postcode search facility to locate your nearest careers centre.

Useful telephone numbers

Contact Careers Scotland for information about this scheme and for general careers advice: 0845 8502 502.

33 Training for Work (Scotland)

Training for Work is a scheme run by Skills Development Scotland (SDS). It has been set up to provide training support for people who are unemployed and actively looking for work. If you live in Scotland, are over the age of 18 and have been unemployed for at least 13 weeks, this scheme may be of interest to you.

This chapter describes the Training for Work scheme and provides information about the amount of money, the eligibility criteria, application procedures and progression routes, concluding with useful websites and contact numbers.

Type of scheme

This scheme has been set up to help people who have been unemployed for some time to take part in vocational training that will improve their chances of getting a job or starting their own business. There is a wide variety of learning programmes that you can access through this scheme, and the programme is backed by local employers who provide on-the-job training. The type of subject areas in which you could receive training include:

- transport and logistics;
- administration and related areas;
- retail and customer service;
- construction and related areas;
- sport, health and social care;
- business counselling;
- food and drink;
- self-employment;
- hospitality and tourism;

- engineering;
- personnel services;
- animal care, land and water based;
- financial services;
- other manufacture.

This training is provided by a variety of training providers across Scotland. If you want to find out more about the courses on offer, and contact details of the training suppliers, use the 'training suppliers directory' available on the Scottish Enterprise website (details below: use the drop down 'programme' menu to click on 'Training for Work' as this will list all the schemes that are available throughout Scotland. Alternatively, you can search by keyword, company name, subject area or geographical area).

The scheme provides the opportunity to work towards Scottish Vocational Qualifications (SVQ) or other job-related qualifications, often combined with actual work experience. For more information about SVQs visit the Scottish Qualifications Authority website (details below). To find out how the variety of qualifications on offer compare with each other visit the Scottish Credit and Qualifications Framework website (details below).

Amount of money

If you choose to take part in this scheme you will be paid a training allowance that is equivalent to your benefits plus an extra £10 a week (2009 figures).

Eligibility criteria

To qualify for the scheme you must meet the following criteria:

- you must live in Scotland;
- you must be over the age of 18;
- you must have been unemployed for at least 13 weeks (in some cases this may be extended to six months, so you should seek clarification from your local Jobcentre Plus).

There may be other exceptions to these rules, so if you do not meet these criteria but think that you could benefit from the scheme, you should seek further advice from your local Jobcentre Plus.

Application procedure

If you are interested in this scheme you should contact your Jobcentre Plus and speak to an adviser who will be able to offer advice about whether this is the most appropriate scheme for your needs. If so, he or she will be able to help you develop your individual plan. This will identify your training requirements and your adviser will be able to put you in touch with a training provider. You can find your nearest Jobcentre by entering your postcode on the Jobcentre Plus website: www.jobcentreplus.gov.uk.

If you would like further information and advice about your career possibilities and the choices that are available before applying to a specific scheme, you can contact Careers Scotland (details below).

Progression routes

This scheme has been designed to help you to move from unemployment into a job or help you to set up your own business. The qualifications and skills that you can gain on the scheme should help you to secure employment, and your work placements should help you to obtain the type of work that interests you. If you are interested in setting up your own business, the training aimed at self-employed people should give you a good grounding in the skills needed to succeed in your business. If you are thinking about becoming self-employed, further information and advice can be obtained from Scottish Enterprise and the Business Gateway (details below).

However, you may also find that you have enjoyed your vocational training course and that you wish to take your learning further, perhaps by enrolling at a further education college or considering some type of work-based learning. For more information about learning and earning schemes in the further education sector, see Part II of this book, and for more information about work-based learning schemes, see Part I.

Further information

Useful websites

www.careers-scotland.org.uk
You can find more information about the Training for Work scheme on this website. You can also find out about other schemes that may be of interest to you, such as Skillseekers, Apprenticeships and the Get Ready for Work scheme (see Chapter 32).

www.skillsdevelopmentscotland.co.uk
Skills Development Scotland was established in 2007. It brings together Careers Scotland, Scottish University for Industry and key skills elements in Scottish Enterprise and Highlands and Islands Enterprise to form a new single skills body. On this website you can find more information about the Training for Work scheme, along with useful links to other organisations that can offer further information and advice about the scheme.

www.scottish-enterprise.com
Scottish Enterprise is Scotland's main economic, enterprise, innovation and investment agency. If you are interested in taking part in the Training for Work scheme to establish your own business in Scotland you can find useful information and advice on this site.

www.sqa.org.uk
This is the website of the Scottish Qualifications Authority, which is the national body in Scotland responsible for the development, accreditation, assessment and certification of qualifications other than degrees. You can find out more about the different qualifications available and you can use the search facility to find information about specific courses.

www.scqf.org.uk
This is the website of the Scottish Credit and Qualifications Framework, which promotes lifelong learning in Scotland and enables people of all ages and circumstances to access education and training. On the website you can find useful information about returning to education and read case studies from adult learners. You can also find out about the different levels of qualifications and information about the number of credits awarded for each of them.

www.salp.org.uk

This is the website of Scotland's Learning Partnership (SLP), which is a national partnership of adult learners and providers in Scotland. The partnership has been set up to help encourage people to take part in adult and family learning. On this website you can obtain more information about the partnership and subscribe to the newsletter, which provides details of adult learning campaigns, projects and schemes available in Scotland.

Useful telephone numbers

Contact Careers Scotland for more information about the Training for Work scheme or for general advice on careers and job-hunting: 0845 8502 502. If you are interested in setting up your own business you can contact the Business Gateway for information and advice: 0845 609 6611.

Training for Success (Northern Ireland)

Training for Success is a scheme available in Northern Ireland for people aged 16–18 (or up to 24 for people who require additional support) to help them to gain the skills and confidence to get a job. The scheme is run by the Department for Employment and Learning and was launched in September 2007, replacing the Jobskills programme. If you are aged 16–18, are not in full-time education or employment and you live in Northern Ireland, this scheme could be of interest to you.

This chapter describes the Training for Success scheme in Northern Ireland and provides information about the amount of money, the eligibility criteria, application procedures and progression routes, concluding with useful websites and contact numbers.

Type of scheme

The Training for Success programme is divided into three components:

1. *Skills for your life:* this component helps you to build on your personal and development skills. It enables you to build your confidence and understanding through a range of cultural, recreational, individual and team activities.
2. *Skills for work:* this component enables you to work towards a Vocationally Relevant Qualification (VRQ) at Level 1, which should help you to obtain a job or enable you to progress to a Pre-Apprenticeship, Apprenticeship or further education. You will also learn about relevant health and safety issues, first aid and information communication technology.
3. *Pre-Apprenticeship:* this component is available for young people who have been assessed as being capable of achieving a VRQ at Level 2, but who have not obtained a job. It is designed for people who are interested

in progressing into employment through the Apprenticeship route. At time of writing, Pre-Apprenticeships are offered in the following sectors:

- hairdressing;
- automotive skills;
- food manufacture;
- environmental and land-based sector;
- travel, tourism and hospitality;
- science, engineering, manufacturing and technology;
- retail;
- building services and engineering.

If you take part in the Training for Success scheme you work together with your training provider to develop a Personal Training Plan that helps to identify your training needs and requirements. You will be able to improve your interview skills and will receive help with job application forms and compiling CVs. You will also take part in job experience and job sampling, based on your needs, which gives you the chance to experience different workplaces and decide what sort of work suits you best. There is also the opportunity to take part in on-the-job training with an employer.

Specialist support

Through the Training for Success scheme there are a number of providers that can supply additional support for individuals who require it (such as those with disabilities) so that they can benefit fully from training. These providers work closely with other training providers to make sure that they can meet the requirements set out in your individual Personal Training Plan. Specialist Support Providers will be able to offer support such as counselling, which will help to improve your confidence, solve personal problems and enable you to progress with your training. They are also able to offer pastoral care, helping to ensure that appropriate child protection and equality policies are provided and observed.

Amount of money

If you train through one of the components of the Training for Success scheme you will qualify automatically for a non-means-tested Education

Maintenance Allowance (EMA) of £40 per week. For more information about the EMA in Northern Ireland, see Chapter 15. Travel, lodging and childcare allowances may be paid depending on your individual circumstances. If you move onto an Apprenticeship, you will be paid the going rate for the job (see Chapter 4 for more information about the Apprenticeship scheme in Northern Ireland).

Benefits

If your parents or guardians receive Income Support, means-tested Job Seeker's Allowance or Housing Benefit, that benefit will not be affected by your £40 EMA payment. If you are entitled to one of these benefits in your own right, your benefit also will not be affected. Your parents or guardians will still be able to receive Child Benefit and Child Tax Credit provided they meet the eligibility requirements.

Eligibility criteria

To be eligible for this scheme you should not be in full-time education or full-time employment, although it is possible to prepare for the scheme when you are about to leave full-time education. You should be aged 16–18 unless you are assessed as having additional needs that could benefit from this programme, in which case the scheme may be open to you up to the age of 24. You need to live in Northern Ireland to take part in this scheme.

Application procedure

If you are interested in this scheme you can find out more information from the contact e-mail addresses and telephone numbers listed below. Alternatively, you can visit a careers adviser at your local Job Centre or Jobs and Benefits Office who will be able to provide more information about the scheme and help you to decide whether it would be suitable for you. They will also be able to provide information about the training organisations that might be able to deliver the training to suit your needs. To obtain contact details of your nearest Job Centre or Jobs and Benefits

Office you can telephone free on 0800 353 530, or you can click on the relevant area highlighted below the map to be found on the Department for Employment and Learning website (details below: enter 'jobs and benefits offices and job centres' into the search box to access the map).

If the scheme is suitable for your needs you will work with a personal adviser to develop your Personal Training Plan. You do not need to complete an application form or attend a selection interview, although learning providers will require a letter from your personal adviser.

Progression routes

This scheme is designed to help young people to find work. Therefore, you might progress from the scheme straight into employment, or you could decide to train as an Apprentice. More information about Apprenticeships in Northern Ireland is provided in Chapter 4.

Other young people find that they have enjoyed their learning and decide to go on to further study, perhaps on a full-time basis at a further education college. There are funds available to help you to study at further education level; these are discussed in Chapter 24. To find out what qualifications are available in Northern Ireland, visit www.qca.org.uk and enter 'Northern Ireland' in the search box to be directed to the relevant part of the site. Here you can find information about National Vocational Qualifications (NVQs) in Northern Ireland.

Further information

Useful websites

www.delni.gov.uk/trainingforsuccess
This section of the Department for Employment and Learning website contains information about the Training for Success scheme in Northern Ireland. There is a section available for young people, employers and training suppliers. Contact details of all the relevant training suppliers can be obtained by clicking on the relevant entry in the table displayed, or you can download a list of approved suppliers from the website.

www.nidirect.gov.uk

This is the official government information website for Northern Ireland citizens. Click on the 'education, learning and skills' section, followed by the 'options after 16' section. This will direct you to the 'Training for Success' section that has information available for young people, employers and training suppliers. This website also contains useful information about obtaining money for your studies, improving your work skills and Apprenticeships.

Training for Success contact details

Tel: (Freephone): 0800 0854 573 (Monday to Friday, 9:00 am to 5:00 pm); Text Freephone: 0800 3280 824 (this is for use by deaf people or those with communication difficulties); Fax: 028 90 441 861; e-mail address: TrainingforSuccess@delni.gov.uk.

35 Programmes for People with Disabilities

There are several schemes available for people with disabilities, or for those who are on health-related benefits, who are looking for paid employment. Most of these schemes involve an element of learning or training, and will provide extra money to help you to develop new skills. These schemes also offer advice and support to help you to return to employment, and some provide additional financial support to help you stay in work. If you have a disability, or you are on health-related benefits and you want to improve your skills to help you to return to work, these schemes will be of interest to you.

This chapter describes the schemes that are available and provides information about the amount of money, the eligibility criteria, application procedures and progression routes, concluding with useful organisations, useful websites, contact numbers and further reading.

Type of scheme

Pathways to Work

Pathways to Work is a scheme run by Jobcentre Plus to encourage people who are in receipt of incapacity benefit because of a health condition or disability to start, or return, to work. In some areas the scheme is delivered by private training providers. You can find a list of these areas by visiting the Jobcentre Plus website (details below). Through this scheme you receive the following help:

- Six focused interviews during the first seven months of claiming incapacity benefit. These help you to identify possible routes into work (including education and training), alert you to the financial benefits that are available and help you to work through the health-related obstacles that may be present. If you do not attend these interviews your benefits may be affected.

- The Condition Management Programme offers education, support and advice on managing your health condition. It is delivered by NHS staff or other specialists and is tailored to meet your needs.
- Payment of a Return to Work Credit. This is a tax-free payment of £40 per week (2009 levels) that is paid to you if you obtain a job that is expected to last at least five weeks and you are working on average over 16 hours a week. To qualify you must earn at least the National Minimum Wage and not be earning over £15,000, gross, per year. (On 1 October 2009 the NWM was set at £5.80 for adult workers aged 22 and over. The development rate for workers aged 18–21 inclusive was set at £4.83 an hour. If you are aged 16 or 17 years old the rate has been set at £3.57.) Also, you must have been in receipt of an incapacity benefit for 13 continuous weeks or more. The credit is payable for up to 52 weeks if you meet these conditions.

More information and advice about this scheme can be obtained from your local Jobcentre, the Jobcentre Plus website (details below) or from the government information website (details below).

New Deal for Disabled People

This scheme is offered in parts of the United Kingdom that are not covered by the Pathways to Work scheme described above. Your local Jobcentre Plus will let you know which scheme is used in your area. The New Deal for Disabled People (NDDP) scheme offers advice and practical support to people on disability and health-related benefits to help them to move from benefits into paid employment.

Through this scheme you work with a 'job broker' who is able to offer guidance and support tailored to your needs. He or she will help you to decide on the best route into employment and work with you to achieve your goals. He or she will also be able to offer advice on obtaining training, producing a CV, applying for jobs and preparing for interviews. Once you have obtained a job he or she will support you during your first six months in work.

More information and advice about this scheme can be obtained from your local Jobcentre, the Jobcentre Plus website (details below) or from the government information website (details below).

Residential training for disabled adults

This scheme provides residential training for disabled adults who are long-term unemployed. Training takes place in nine specialist colleges (with accessible buildings and fully qualified, experienced staff) located throughout England. Although there are no specialist colleges in other parts of the United Kingdom, any eligible UK-based adult can apply. For a list of residential training providers, and to obtain contact details, visit the 'disabled people' section on www.direct.gov.uk and click on 'employment support'. There are over 50 courses of vocational training available, with many leading to National Vocational Qualifications (NVQs). More information about this scheme can be obtained from your local Jobcentre Plus or from the Residential Training Unit (details below). For more information about NVQs, see Chapter 21.

Work preparation programme

This is a programme run by Jobcentre Plus to help people return to work after a long period of sickness or unemployment. The scheme helps you to identify work opportunities, gain work experience in a work environment, learn new skills or update old skills, and helps to build your confidence. The programme usually lasts between six and 13 weeks and takes place locally, either at the premises of a programme provider or a local workplace.

More information and advice about this scheme can be obtained from your local Jobcentre, the Jobcentre Plus website (details below) or from the government information website (details below).

WORKSTEP

This is an employment programme that helps people with disabilities obtain and retain a job. It is managed by Jobcentre Plus, which works with around 180 local authorities, voluntary and private sector organisations and Remploy (details below), to provide support so that eligible disabled people can work, develop and progress in a wide range of jobs. The scheme is tailored to your individual needs and offers practical assistance to employers to make sure that they can meet these needs.

More information and advice about this scheme can be obtained from your local Jobcentre, the Jobcentre Plus website (details below) or from the government information website (details below). In Northern Ireland the scheme is known as Steps to Work; visit www.dsdni.gov.uk for more information.

Access to Work scheme

This scheme has been set up to help employers meet the costs associated with employing a person with special needs. It will pay for specialist equipment and will also pay for a communicator at job interviews. You may be able to use funds from this scheme to help to pay for specialist equipment that you require on a training course. More information and advice about this scheme can be obtained from your local Jobcentre, the Jobcentre Plus website (details below) or from the government information website (details below).

Amount of money

You will continue to receive your usual benefits while you are looking for work. Once in employment you may qualify for a Return to Work Credit of £40 per week, in addition to your wages paid by your employer. The Return to Work Credit will not affect any amount you are paid for Council Tax Benefit, Housing Benefit, Working Tax Credit and Child Tax Credit. Also, it will not affect the amount you pay in Income Tax and National Insurance Contributions. You can claim from the date you start work or become self-employed, but you must make your claim within five weeks from the date you start work. Your local Jobcentre Plus office will pay the credit to you each week directly into your bank, building society or Post Office account.

If you take part in the residential training scheme you will receive an allowance during your training. Your residential costs, which can also include some travel costs, will be paid for by the Residential Training Unit. You will also be able to continue receiving your benefits while you are on the residential training programme.

For the WORKSTEP, work preparation and access to work schemes you will continue to receive your benefits, until you obtain a job, when you will begin to receive your salary.

Eligibility criteria

Pathways to Work

You can apply for help from Pathways to Work if you are entitled to certain benefits because of your health condition or a disability. These include the following:

- Employment and Support Allowance (this replaced Incapacity Benefit and Income Support, paid because of an illness or disability, for new claims from 27 October 2008);
- Incapacity Benefit;
- Income Support on the grounds of incapacity;
- Income Support while you are appealing against a decision that you are not incapable of work;
- Severe Disablement Allowance.

New Deal for Disabled People

This scheme is available for people who are in receipt of one or more of the following benefits:

- Employment and Support Allowance;
- Incapacity Benefit;
- Severe Disablement Allowance;
- Income Support including a disability premium;
- Income Support because your Incapacity Benefit has been stopped and you are appealing against the decision;
- National Insurance credits because of incapacity;
- Disability Living Allowance, provided you are not in receipt of Jobseeker's Allowance and are not in paid work for 16 hours or more a week;

- Housing Benefit with a disability premium, provided you are not in receipt of Jobseeker's Allowance and are not in paid work for 16 hours or more a week;
- Council Tax Benefit, provided you are not in receipt of Jobseeker's Allowance and are not in paid work for 16 hours or more a week;
- War Pension with an Unemployability Supplement;
- Industrial Injuries Disablement Benefit with an Unemployability Supplement;
- a benefit equivalent to Incapacity Benefit from a European Union (EU) member country.

Residential training for disabled adults

You will qualify for the residential training scheme if you meet the following conditions:

- you are a UK resident;
- you have a physical or sensory disability, or a learning difficulty;
- you are aged 18 or over;
- you cannot access suitable local training;
- you are unemployed and have the potential to take up employment, including supported employment.

Work preparation programme

To take part on this scheme you will need to be thinking about returning to work after a long period of sickness or unemployment. Your Disability Employment Adviser (DEA) at your Jobcentre Plus will be able to offer advice about whether you are eligible and advise you as to whether the scheme is the most appropriate for your needs.

WORKSTEP

To take part in this scheme you will need to be thinking about getting a job in which you will work for at least 16 hours a week. Your DEA will be able to offer advice about whether you are eligible and advise you as to whether the scheme is the most appropriate for your needs.

Access to Work scheme

To take part in this scheme you can be unemployed and about to start a job or a work trial, or you can already be employed or self-employed. Your disability or health condition must be such that it stops you from being able to do some parts of your job or training so that you need extra help, support or equipment. Your disability or health condition may not have a big effect on what you do each day, but may have a long-term effect on how well you can do your job or carry out your training. Your DEA will be able to offer advice about whether this scheme is the most appropriate for your needs.

Application procedure

If you are claiming incapacity benefits for the first time, or are claiming again after a break in receiving benefit, you will be considered automatically for the Pathways to Work scheme. Alternatively, you can volunteer for the programme. Contact your Jobcentre for more information and advice.

To take part on the NDDP visit your local Jobcentre to find out whether the scheme is available in your area. If it is, you can find a local job broker by visiting www.jobbrokersearch.co.uk. You may find it useful to talk to several job brokers so that you can find a person you get on with and who can offer you the help you require. Once you have found a suitable job broker you can register with them and arrange your first appointment. You can leave the NDDP scheme at any time.

To apply for residential training, the work preparation programme, WORK-STEP or Access to Work contact your DEA at your local Jobcentre. He or she will look at the options available and put you forward for the most suitable programme, helping you with any application forms that may be required.

Progression routes

All these schemes are designed to help you move from benefits into paid employment. You can gain new skills that will help you to make progress in the workplace, perhaps taking on more responsibility, applying for new jobs in the future and increasing your salary. All the schemes will offer additional support once you have started work. This will ensure that your needs are being met by your employer and that you are receiving the required support.

If you choose to take part in the residential training programme or any other education and training you will be able to learn new skills and gain nationally recognised qualifications that could help you to secure a job or go on to further study. If you are interested in study at further education level, see Part II of this book and if you are interested in study at higher education level, see Part III. There are additional funds available for people with disabilities who wish to study at college and university. These are called Disabled Students' Allowances (DSAs), which are funds set up by the government to help you with extra costs you may have to pay as a result of your disability. The funds will pay for non-medical personal help, major items of specialist equipment, travel and other course-related costs. DSAs are not dependent on your income or that of your parents. Students with disabilities are also eligible to apply for other forms of government funding, such as student loans, Special Support Grants and hardship funds. More information about DSAs and other types of funding for students at higher education level can be found in Dawson, C (2009) *The Essential Guide to Paying for University: Effective funding strategies for parents and students*, London: Kogan Page (£9.99).

Further information

Useful organisations

If you are interested in finding out more about the residential training programme, contact the Residential Training Unit:

Residential Training Unit
Government Office for the North East, Citygate, Gallowgate,
Newcastle upon Tyne NE1 4WH
Tel: (0191) 202 3579; Fax: (0191) 202 3626; e-mail: rtu@gone.gsi.gov.uk

Useful websites

www.jobcentreplus.gov.uk
Jobcentre Plus is a government agency that is part of the Department for Work and Pensions (DWP). Its role is to support people of working age

from welfare into work and to help to fill vacancies advertised by employers. This website contains information about all the schemes that are available for people with disabilities. You can use the postcode search on the website to find contact details of your nearest Jobcentre Plus office.

www.remploy.co.uk
Remploy is one of the UK's leading providers of employment services and employment for people with disabilities. Remploy has a network of town and city centre branches that are available to offer support and advice. Contact details can be obtained from the website, along with information about the services offered to people who are out of work and claiming disability, sickness or incapacity benefits.

Useful telephone numbers

Remploy can be contacted on 0845 601 5878.

Further reading

If you are interested in studying at further or higher education level, a booklet called *Bridging the Gap* answers most questions about DSAs. It can be downloaded from the relevant Student Finance website:

England: www.studentfinanceengland.co.uk
Wales: www.studentfinancewales.co.uk
Northern Ireland: www.studentfinanceni.co.uk
Scotland: www.saas.gov.uk

Alternatively, it can be obtained from your LA or by phoning 0800 731 9133. The booklet is available in Braille, large print and on audio tape.

36 In Work Credits and Job Grants

In Work Credits are available for single parents who are bringing up children alone and start working more than 16 hours a week. Job Grants are available for people who have been unemployed for more than six months who start a job working more than 16 hours a week. You can receive both these payments when undertaking in-house training for your job and both schemes are available in all parts of the United Kingdom. If you are moving from benefits to employment and are intending to work for more than 16 hours a week, these schemes may be of interest to you.

This chapter describes the In Work Credits and Job Grant schemes and provides information about the amount of money, the eligibility criteria, application procedures and progression routes, concluding with useful websites and contact numbers.

Type of scheme

Both of these schemes have been designed to help make the transition from unemployment to work easier, in terms of financial pressures. They are aimed at people who have been unemployed for six months or more (Job Grant) and claiming benefits for 52 weeks or more (In Work Credit). The In Work Credit scheme is only available for lone parents. You can continue to receive payments if you undertake in-house training for your job.

Amount of money

The amount of Job Grant you will get depends on your circumstances, and is paid at the following rates (2009 figures): £100 for single people, couples and civil partnerships without children; and £250 for lone parents, couples and civil partnerships with children.

The Job Grant is tax-free and does not affect other benefits or tax credits you may be entitled to once you start work. Also, if you qualify for the Job Grant you will be eligible for Extended Council Tax Benefit and Extended Housing Benefit (see below). More information about these benefits can be obtained from the government information website (www.direct.gov.uk), from your local benefits office or from your local Jobcentre Plus office.

The In Work Credit is a fixed tax-free payment of £40 per week (£60 per week in London) for parents bringing up children alone. It is payable for up to 52 weeks on top of your earnings, when you start work of at least 16 hours per week.

Additional funds

You may also be able to qualify for additional financial help, depending on your current financial circumstances. This could include Housing Benefit and Council Tax Benefit paid at the same rate (if you are currently in receipt of these benefits) for the first four weeks of your new work arrangements. If you are getting help with mortgage interest paid with your Income Support or income-based Jobseeker's Allowance, you may be able to get this paid for the first four weeks that you are in work. If you are a lone parent you may be able to obtain additional help of up to £300. This is called the in-work emergency discretion fund, which can help you to cope with unexpected financial problems that could stop you continuing in your job. The fund only makes discretionary payments and your Jobcentre Plus personal adviser makes the decision about whether you should get the money. Other funds may be available to help you to pay for the cost of travel to interviews and to buy clothes for interviews and for work.

To find out whether you would qualify for any of this additional financial help, contact your personal adviser at your Jobcentre Plus. It is advisable to do this before you start work as some schemes will need you to complete and return the application form before your work commences.

Eligibility criteria

You may be eligible for a Job Grant if you have been claiming Employment and Support Allowance, Incapacity Benefit, Income Support, Jobseeker's Allowance or Severe Disablement Allowance continuously for more than six months and are starting work of more than 16 hours per week. You may also get the Job Grant if your partner or civil partner starts working at least 24 hours a week and your benefits stop because he or she is working.

To claim the In Work Credit you must be bringing up children on your own, intending to start work of at least 16 hours a week and expect that work to last five weeks or more. You must also have been getting Income Support or Jobseeker's Allowance or a combination of these benefits for at least 52 weeks or more without a break.

Application procedure

You do not need to apply for a Job Grant as you will receive it automatically if you are eligible when you start work. However, you must tell your Jobcentre Plus office that you are starting work. The grant is paid in the same way as your benefits are paid.

The In Work Credit must be claimed before you start work. Speak to your personal adviser at your local Jobcentre Plus before you start your job to receive an application form. The form must be completed and returned to your nearest Jobcentre Plus office within five weeks of starting work.

Progression routes

Both these scheme have been designed to ease financial pressures on people moving from benefits to paid employment. Once these worries have been reduced, you may find that you are able to progress further within your job, or you might be able to look for other, perhaps better paid jobs. Some employers will offer in-house or external training to help you to carry out your work more effectively and efficiently, and taking part in one of these schemes could help you to apply for other jobs in the future, or may lead to promotion with your existing employer. There is a variety of schemes available to help you to take part in work-based learning while you are earning a wage; these are discussed in Part I of this book.

Further information

Useful websites

www.jobcentreplus.gov.uk
Jobcentre Plus is a government agency that helps people of working age to move from benefits into work, and helps employers to fill their vacancies. On this website you can use the search facility to find a job. You can search the database by type of job, keyword or job reference number. You can also use a quick search facility to find out more about the type of work that is available in the area in which you live. Information is also available on training, careers, childcare and voluntary work.

http://jobseekers.direct.gov.uk
You can look for jobs, training, careers, childcare and voluntary work using the search facility on this site. You can search by job type and geographical location. Each entry contains a description of the job, wages, working hours, date posted, pension details, application procedures and employer contact details.

www.jobcentreonline.com
If you live in Northern Ireland you can use this site to find job vacancies in your area. You can search the database using the quick search facility, by job category, and you can narrow and refine your search by region, wage band, full/part-time and temporary/permanent position.

www.adviceguide.org.uk
This is the information and advice website of the Citizens Advice Bureau. Visit the relevant part of the site for your country to obtain information about benefits and job grants when you start work.

Useful telephone numbers

If you need to make a claim for benefits, you can do so by calling Jobcentre Plus on 0800 055 6688.

If you want to find out about job vacancies in your area, you can do so by phoning Jobcentre Plus on 0845 6060 234.

37 New Deal

New Deal is a range of programmes designed to help adults who have been out of work for long or short periods of time. Through these programmes you are offered careers advice and guidance and given the opportunity to take part in education, training or work experience designed to help you get back into work. Additional grants or allowances may be available while you train or when you enter work. If you are unemployed and hoping to improve your chances of gaining work, this scheme may be of interest to you.

This chapter describes the various New Deal schemes that are available and provides information about the amount of money, the eligibility criteria, application procedures and progression routes, concluding with useful websites and contact numbers.

Type of scheme

There are several New Deal programmes currently available. However, they are being replaced in some areas from October 2009 by the Flexible New Deal programme, which is described in more detail below.

New Deal for Young People

This programme has been designed for people aged 18–24 who have been unemployed and claiming Jobseeker's Allowance for six months or more. If you have been unemployed for more than six months you must take part in this programme, otherwise your benefits may be affected.

The first part of the programme is called the 'gateway' period. It offers intensive training in employability skills for up to four months. After this period, if you have not obtained a job, you take part in the second part of the programme, called 'options'. This will last at least 13 weeks and provides the opportunity to take part in training and work experience. The final stage of the programme is offered to people who still have not obtained a job, and is called 'follow-through'. This stage can last up to 26 weeks and provides you with additional help and support in finding a job.

New Deal 25 plus

This scheme is available for people over the age of 25 but under State pension age who have been out of work for at least 18 months. It is split into three stages (similar to those described above) that are designed to enhance employment prospects by providing intensive training to update and improve your skills. You are also given help in searching for jobs and offered specialist careers guidance. You must take part in this programme if you have been unemployed for more than 18 months, otherwise your benefits could be affected.

In some areas of England, 'Employment Zone' is delivered instead of New Deal. It is a similar scheme to New Deal 25 plus, offering you advice and guidance to help get back into work. Your personal adviser at your local Jobcentre will be able to let you know whether New Deal or Employment Zone is delivered in your area. Alternatively, visit the Jobcentre Plus website for a list of counties in which Employment Zone is delivered (details below).

New Deal 50 plus

Through this voluntary scheme older people are offered practical advice and help in getting back to work or setting up their own business. You can join this scheme if you have been in receipt of one of the following benefits for at least six months:

- Income Support;
- Jobseeker's Allowance;
- Incapacity Benefit;
- Severe Disablement Allowance;
- Pension Credit.

You may also be able to join the scheme if you have been getting National Insurance credits or Carer's Allowance, or if your partner has been in receipt of other benefits for you for at least six months. A training grant may be payable when you enter work or self-employment.

New Deal for Disabled People

If you have a disability or long-term illness, this scheme is designed to be of benefit to you. Through this voluntary scheme you are offered the service of a job broker that has been chosen because of their experience of working with people with disabilities. Job brokers are a mix of private, voluntary and public organisations that work with Jobcentre Plus across the United Kingdom. They will help you to access a network of education and training opportunities, offer advice and guidance about employment and liaise with employers on your behalf. You can find a job broker in your area by visiting www.jobbrokersearch.gov.uk.

There are other types of scheme available if you have a disability; these are discussed in Chapter 35.

New Deal for Lone Parents

This voluntary scheme offers help for lone parents to get back into work. It is available for lone parents with children under the age of 16 who are working less than 16 hours a week or not working at all. Through this scheme you could qualify for financial help towards your education and training, especially to cover childcare costs. There are other childcare schemes available, depending on the type of education, training and work experience that you undertake; these are described in Chapter 23.

New Deal for Partners

If your partner is currently claiming benefits you could join this voluntary scheme to help you to find work. A 'partner' can be a husband, wife or civil partner, or someone you live with as if they were such. This scheme is available if your partner is claiming any of the following:

- Jobseeker's Allowance;
- Income Support;
- Incapacity Benefit;

- Carer's Allowance;
- Severe Disablement Benefit;
- Pension Credit.

You can also join New Deal for Partners if your partner gets Pension Credit and you are working less than 24 hours a week, or if you or your partner gets Working Tax Credit and you are working less than 16 hours a week. Through this scheme you will receive help, advice, training and education and could receive financial help for childcare.

New Deal for Musicians

If you are interested in becoming a musician, this scheme helps to put you in touch with a mentor working within the music industry. They are able to offer advice and guidance on getting into the industry. To take part in New Deal for musicians, you must be taking part in New Deal 25 plus or New Deal for Young People, and at the end of the 'gateway' stage (see above). Also, you will need to have already worked in the music industry, or have music qualifications and/or live in an area with few or no music facilities. You must have some experience as an instrumentalist, singer, song writer, DJ or composer.

Flexible New Deal

In April 2009 the Chancellor, Alastair Darling, announced that there would be additional support for long-term jobseekers through the Flexible New Deal (FND) programme. The intention is that, from October 2009, the programmes discussed above will be replaced by the FND programme in some areas of the United Kingdom. This will offer work and training through private or voluntary sector contractors to people who have been unemployed for more than 12 months. Your personal adviser will be able to tell you whether the new scheme is being introduced in your area.

At time of writing there are some concerns about the scheme. For example, some experts warn that there is not enough funding in place to ensure that the scheme can go ahead, because, due to the recession, there are three times as many applicants as was originally predicted. More information about the introduction and progress of this scheme can be obtained from the Jobcentre Plus website (details below).

Amount of money

You will continue to receive your usual benefits when you begin the New Deal programme. If you move to the second stage of the programme you will receive the New Deal Allowance, which is the same amount as your Jobseeker's Allowance, plus a weekly top-up sum. Your other benefits are not affected by this allowance. Also, you may be able to receive financial help for travel to interviews and for childcare.

People who take part in the New Deal 50 plus scheme can apply for a training grant of up to £1,200 for training that is related to their job, or up to £300 for general training courses. You can apply for this training grant at any time in the first two years of starting your job (this also applies to setting up your own business).

New Deal programmes are designed to make sure that you are better off in work than you are on benefits, so you should be able to earn more money than you currently receive in benefits once you are in employment. Your personal adviser will be able to tell you more about the amount of money that you could earn in employment and which of your benefits may or may not be affected when you find work. For example, you may be able to receive help with mortgage interest payments, Council Tax and rent for the first few weeks in work (see Chapter 36 for more information about this scheme). Once you start work you may also be eligible for Working Tax Credits and Child Tax Credits, which can help to boost your income further. More information about Tax Credits can be obtained from www.taxcredits.inlandrevenue.gov.uk.

Eligibility criteria

To take part in the New Deal programme you must meet the eligibility criteria specific to your programme, in terms of age, disability and the length of time that you have been unemployed. In some cases, however, you may be able to join the New Deal programme if you have been unemployed for a shorter period of time. Speak to your adviser at your local Jobcentre Plus to find out whether you are eligible for the New Deal scheme.

Application procedure

If you are required to take part in one of the New Deal schemes because you have been unemployed for some time, your personal adviser will make this clear and illustrate how your benefits could be affected if you decide not to participate. He or she will place you on the scheme and work with you to make sure that it is meeting your needs.

If you wish to attend one of the voluntary New Deal schemes, speak to your personal adviser at your local Jobcentre Plus office to find out whether the scheme is appropriate for your needs. If so, he or she will make arrangements for you and work with you to make sure that the scheme is meeting your requirements.

Progression routes

New Deal schemes are designed to help you to move from unemployment and claiming benefits into paid employment. Through this programme you will work with an adviser who will help you to achieve this goal. You may also decide to take part in further education and training to help you to secure work. More information about learning and earning schemes that are available in the further education sector can be found in Part II of this book. Alternatively, once you have found work you may be interested in continuing your training through some type of work-based learning. These schemes are described in Part I of this book.

Further information

Useful websites

www.jobcentreplus.gov.uk
Further information about the New Deal programme can be obtained from this website. You can also find the contact details of your local Jobcentre Plus offices by using the postcode search facility available on this site. Leaflets for each type of New Deal scheme are available for download.

http://nextstep.direct.gov.uk

Nextstep is a free service that offers face-to-face help and support on training, learning and employment for people living in England. You can use the nextstep service if you are aged 20 or over, or aged 18 or 19 and have been referred to nextstep by Jobcentre Plus. On this site you can obtain contact details of your nearest nextstep office. Contact them direct for tailor-made information and advice.

www.adviceguide.org.uk

This is the information and advice website of the Citizens Advice Bureau (CAB). Visit the relevant part of the site for your country to obtain information and advice about New Deal and other government employment schemes that may be suitable for your needs. Alternatively, you can visit your local CAB office for advice about schemes and information about how they may affect your benefits.

www.careers-scotland.org.uk

If you live in Scotland, visit this website for more information about choosing and applying for jobs. You can use the Careers Match Scotland service available on this site to help you to find the type of job that would suit you.

www.careerswales.com

If you live in Wales, visit this site for more information about choosing and finding a job. You can use the 'careers ideas' section of the site to help you to find out more about the type of jobs that are available, including the level of pay, qualifications required and what the job involves. The service is available in English and Welsh.

www.careersserviceni.com

If you live in Northern Ireland visit this site for more information about finding and applying for a job. The website contains contact details of careers services throughout Northern Ireland, along with comprehensive advice about writing a CV and a covering letter. There are also useful tips about filling in application forms and attending a job interview.

Useful telephone numbers

You can contact Jobcentre Plus to find out what jobs are available in your area on 0845 6060 234 (textphone 0845 6055 255).

If you live in Northern Ireland, the Careers Service Support Unit can be contacted on 028 9044 1781.

If you live in Scotland, the Careers Scotland helpline is 0845 850 2502.

If you live in England or Wales, you can obtain careers advice by phoning 0800 100 900.

Appendix 1: Case Studies

Case study 1: Nadine

Nadine is 18 years old and left school with one GSCE in Art and Design. She finished school in the summer of 2007 but has been unable to obtain a job since then. Over the last four months she has been working on the New Deal programme where she has been given the opportunity to work closely with an adviser who has arranged for her to attend various courses and workshops that will help her to apply for jobs. This has included a workshop in which Nadine has been able to produce a CV. She says:

> It's good. I didn't know I'd got all that stuff, you know, done all that stuff that I could put down. You know, they said looking after me brother could go down, you know, like feeding him and changing him and everything. You know, like it might help with, if I wanted to do a job with children, like in a nursery or something... So they showed me how to do that. 'Cos I've looked after him since he was a baby and now he's 5 and I don't think I've done a bad job. He's a good boy really... So I might be able to go for a job with kids, they've shown me that. I didn't know that. I was looking at art and things, you know, 'cos of my exam, but I couldn't get anything like that.

Since moving to the second stage of the New Deal programme, Nadine has received an extra allowance to help her with additional costs associated with her training, which has included work experience in a local nursery. Nadine says:

> Yeah, it's been good. You know, they're nice people down there. But yeah, the money's really helped. 'Cos I had to get the bus there, so they helped me with that, 'cos it's £1.20 there and back every day. So I liked that and I've learnt some new stuff, you know, but I did most of that

with me brother anyway. I think I could do that for a job… Next week I'm going to another place so that should be good as well.

Nadine hopes that her training and work experience will lead to a job working with children. Although she has applied for four jobs recently, as yet she has not been called for an interview. However, she says:

I hope I do get an interview 'cos we've done that on the course. We've learnt how to answer the questions, you know, plan for the questions, what they might ask, like, why do you want this job and what are your skills? So I can say what I've done, work experience and looking after me brother and all that, you know… so I hope I do get an interview soon.

Overall, Nadine believes that the New Deal programme has helped her and she has found the extra money very useful:

I thought they might stop me benefits or something, but they didn't and then I got more money, because I was doing all that training and work and stuff, and that was good 'cos money's tight. Yeah, I'm glad I've done it really, I do want to get a job and I think this will help me.

For information about the New Deal for Young People programme, see Chapter 37.

Case study 2: Kathryn

Kathryn lives in Cardiff and sent the following by e-mail:

I am 24 years old and have lived in Cardiff all my life. I left school as soon as I could; to be honest I did not like it and wanted to leave and get a job to earn some money. I worked as an assistant in a hairdressers until I fell pregnant with Evann (my first child!) I stopped work to look after him but now he has gone to school full time I felt like I had to get out and do something, not anything but something worthwhile. I wanted to go back to college but I was not really sure what I wanted to do so I went to my local careers place and the lady told me about these grants I could get because I am on benefits and I did not get any qualifications at school. It is called the Individual Learning Account and I got £200 to spend on a course leading to a qualification and I can use it to help me get a job, so I went back to the hairdressers to work part time and then I went to college in the evening when Owen could look after the children (he is my husband!) I went to study English and maths gcse [sic] because so many jobs ask for those two subjects. I finish both of them this year and my tutor thinks I am going to (do) really well. I like learning now because they are all adults in the class and we have a good laugh, it is very different to what it was at school where we did not have a laugh at all! I have been told that I can maybe get another £200 next year if I want to carry on and I think I do because I would like to study something like child care. It is good for me because it helps to pay for learning something new and I might not have paid it for myself because I might have thought I was wasting my money. But now I know I was not wasting my money at all!

For information about Individual Learning Accounts in Wales, see Chapter 16.

Case study 3: Marcus

Marcus is 16 years old and leaves school this summer. He has always wanted to be a car mechanic and has decided that the best route into this job is through becoming an apprentice. His mother, Sarah, feels that he is a very determined boy and that he will succeed on the Apprenticeship:

He's known all along he wanted to work with cars. He's had a heap of engine parts in the garage for the last five years. I shouldn't be facetious – it's actually a go-kart he and his brother have been building and it does actually work although I won't let them take it anywhere near the road. He's really good at it and he's very determined... We weren't really surprised when he came home from school and told us he'd already got this Apprenticeship sorted out. It's with a company on the Granby (the local industrial estate) so he can walk to work. Although I know he'll take his test as soon as he can. He can drive already anyway... Well, we're very pleased. You hear of these kids who just don't know what they want to do when they leave school. So we're very lucky with Marcus.

Marcus arranged the Apprenticeship himself after having had discussions with his careers teacher at school. He was put in touch with the local employer and went to visit the site, where he had to undertake an interview and a practical test that involved the identification of various car parts. Marcus says:

> It was easy. I knew all that. And the interview was ok as well. I liked him (the owner of the garage). He's got his own Ford Mustang out the back. Yeah, it'll be better than school. And I can have my own garage one day.

Sarah has no doubts that this will be the case. She laughs and says:

> He may not be very communicative, but he will be an excellent car mechanic. And we have no doubt that he will own his own garage one day. His dad's self-employed, I think it's in the blood. But it's great he can do these Apprenticeships now. Although he's a clever boy, university would never be right for him. He's too practical and he's almost hyperactive, always on the go. So I think this Apprenticeship will be excellent for him. And it will keep him busy and off the streets.

For information about the Apprenticeship scheme in different parts of the United Kingdom see Chapters 1, 2, 3 and 4.

Case study 4: Anita

Anita works in a hospital, teaching children who are too ill to go to school. Although the job can be a little upsetting at times, she describes it as 'the best job in the world', and she 'wouldn't change it for anything'. However, Anita lives on her own and found that her evenings could be 'a little boring' especially with 'all the rubbish on television'. She decided that she would like to study during the evenings, while she was still working and receiving a good wage.

After researching the opportunities locally, which she felt 'were rather limited', she decided that an Open University (OU) course would be best. This provided a wide variety of courses and would enable her to study at her own pace and at a time that suited her. Also, it would mean that she would not have to commit herself to regular attendance at classes, which could be problematic, especially 'during the cold winter months'.

Anita completed her course last year, graduating with a degree in Law from the OU. She found that the course had been very affordable, but understood that a new ruling had come into place that would make it very difficult for her to afford such a course in the future. (This new ruling stated that from 2008/09 funding would no longer be provided to students who study for a qualification that is equivalent to, or lower than, a qualification they already hold. This means that universities will have to decide whether to raise their tuition fees for this type of student because they will receive no extra funding from the government. However, certain courses will be exempt from this policy, such as teacher-training, nursing and social work. Anita already had a degree from Liverpool John Moores University and, therefore, under the new rules, would not qualify for state funding for her Law degree. This means that the cost of this type of course would now be far too high for Anita. It is believed that the OU, in particular, will be hit hard by this new ruling.)

Although Anita doesn't intend changing her paid employment, she thinks that she will be able to put her new qualification 'to good use' in her capacity as a volunteer at the local Citizens Advice Bureau.

For information about part-time learning opportunities with the Open University and other providers, see Chapter 25.

Case study 5: James and Richard

James and Richard are 15-year-old twins who are about to take their GCSEs. Their mother reports that they have been working hard and are both expected to get good grades. However, initially neither boy was sure about what they wanted to do after their GSCEs, despite their mother trying to persuade them to stay on at school and study for their A levels. It was only after they found out that they would qualify for the Education Maintenance Allowance (EMA) that they were persuaded to stay on, as their mother recalls:

> Left to their own devices they would leave school and try to get a job so they can pay for their football and speedway. That seems to be all that interests them. But I kept telling them they would stand a better chance of getting a job if they got their A levels. Both their older brothers

have gone to university, but the twins just lack that drive. They want money but they don't know how they're going to get it... When their brothers were at school Peter had a better job so they didn't qualify for the EMA, but then Peter was made redundant, well, he took voluntary redundancy, so now the twins will qualify for the £30 a week... Well, when I told them you should have seen their faces. I told them the money was for them and they could spend it how they wanted. That will pay for their football and their speedway, every week, for the whole year. They suddenly thought staying on was the best thing ever... I know money shouldn't act as an incentive but I'm glad it has with them. I think when they get down to it they'll like their studies... Maybe they might want to go to university as well. Who knows?

For information about the EMA in different parts of the United Kingdom, see Chapters 12, 13, 14 and 15.

Appendix 2: Overview of Scheme Payments

Below is a summary of the amounts of money that are available through the various learning and earning schemes described in this book (2009 figures), arranged alphabetically:

Type of scheme	Amount of money
Access to Work (disabilities)	usual benefits then salary once in work
Adult Learning Grant	£10 – £30 per week
Apprenticeships	minimum of £80 per week minimum of £50 per week for FMA in Wales
BTEC and OCR Nationals	your usual wage or benefits plus possible training allowance or discretionary funds (various amounts)
Care to Learn (England)	up to £160 per child per week (£175 in London)
Career Development Loans	£300 – £8,000 loan, depending on need
Childcare Grant (HE)	maximum of £148.75 per week for one child and £255 for two children (England and Northern Ireland); £161.50 per week for one child and £274.55 per week for two or more children (Wales)
Childcare in Scotland	various amounts depending on need and available funds

Childcare Support Fund (from colleges)	various amounts depending on need and available funds
City & Guild bursaries	various amounts, depending on need
Company sponsorship	£300 – £9,000 per year depending on type of sponsorship and contract
Discretionary support funds	various amounts depending on need and available funds
EMA	£10 – £30 per week plus periodic bonuses
Entrepreneurship and self-employment	various, depending on type and success of business
Entry to Employment (England)	£30 a week
FE Awards (Northern Ireland)	up to 85 per cent of childcare costs, up to a maximum of £185 a week for one child and £300 for two or more children
Gap years	the usual wage for the job
Get Ready for Work (Scotland)	minimum of £55 per week
In Work Credit	fixed tax-free payment of £40 per week (£60 per week in London) for parents bringing up children alone
Individual Learning Accounts	up to £100 or £200 per year (Wales) up to £200 or £500 per year (Scotland)
Investors in People	your usual wage
Job grant	£100 – £250 one-off payment
Learning through Work	your usual wage
National Vocational Qualifications	your usual wage or benefits plus possible training allowance or discretionary funds (various amounts)

New Deal	usual benefits plus training allowance in second stage of scheme; training grant of up to £1,200 for training (job-related), or up to £300 training (general) for New Deal 50 plus participants
Parents' Learning Allowance (HE)	maximum of £1,508 per year
Part-time grant	up to £1,210 plus £260 (England and Northern Ireland); up to £955 plus £1,075 (Wales); up to £500 (Scotland)
Part-time learning	your usual wage or benefits plus relevant grants
Pathways to Work (disabilities)	£40 per week Return to Work Credit
Professional loans	up to £25,000
Professional training	the usual qualified/unqualified wage for the job plus possible grants and bursaries and extra money for work placements and travel
Residential training (disabilities)	usual benefits plus training allowance
Sixth Form Childcare Scheme (England)	up to £160 per child per week (£175 in London)
Skill Build (Wales)	minimum of £50 per week
Skillseekers (Scotland)	minimum of £55 per week
Student part-time and vacation work	at least the minimum wage: £5.80 an hour for workers aged 22 and over; £4.83 for workers aged 18–21; £3.57 for workers aged 16 or 17
Time off for Study	your usual wage
Trade union funding	various amounts

Train to Gain	your usual wage
Training for Success (Northern Ireland)	£40 per week
Training for Work (Scotland)	usual benefits plus training allowance
University bursaries	various amounts, depending on the university policy
Work placements	the usual wage for the job plus possible grant from the university/college and reduced tuition fees
Work preparation (disabilities)	usual benefits then salary once in work
WORKSTEP (disabilities)	usual benefits then salary once in work

Further Information

Useful organisations

Funding for healthcare and social work

For enquiries concerning NHS and social work financial support in England contact:

Student Grants Unit
Hesketh House, 200–220 Broadway, Fleetwood, Lancashire FY7 8SS
Tel: 0845 358 6655; Fax: 01253 774490; e-mail: bursary@nhspa.gov.uk; website: www.nhsstudentgrants.co.uk

For enquiries concerning NHS financial support in Wales contact:

The NHS Wales Student Awards Unit
3rd Floor, 14 Cathedral Road, Cardiff CF11 9LJ
Tel: 029 2019 6167 (bursary enquiries); Tel: 029 2019 6168 (childcare enquiries); e-mail: use contact form on website: www.nliah.com

For enquiries concerning NHS financial support in Scotland contact:

The Student Awards Agency for Scotland
3 Redheughs Rigg, South Gyle, Edinburgh EH12 9HH
Tel: 0845 111 1711; Fax: 0131 244 5887; e-mail: use contact form on website: www.saas.gov.uk

For enquiries concerning NHS financial support in Northern Ireland contact:

Central Services Agency
Bursary Administration Unit, Nursing Board NI, 2 Franklin Street, Belfast BT2 8 DQ
Tel. 028 9055 3661; e-mail: use contact form on website: www.centralservicesagency.com

If you live in Wales contact the Care Council for Wales for more information about funding for social work:

Student Funding Team
7th Floor, South Gate House, Wood Street, Cardiff CF10 1EW
Tel: 0845 070 0249; e-mail: studentfunding@ccwales.org.uk;
website: www.ccwales.org.uk

If you live in Scotland contact the Scottish Social Services Council for more information about social work:

Compass House
11 Riverside Drive, Dundee DD1 4NY
Tel: 0845 60 30 891; e-mail: enquiries@sssc.uk.com;
website: www.sssc.uk.com

If you live in Northern Ireland contact the Northern Ireland Social Care Council (NISCC) for more information about social work:

Northern Ireland Social Care Council (NISCC)
7th Floor, Millennium House, 19–25 Great Victoria Street, Belfast BT2 7AQ
Tel: 028 9041 7600; Fax: 028 9041 7601;
e-mail: info@nisocialcarecouncil.org.uk; website: www.niscc.info

Trade union funding

The Communication Workers' Union can be contacted at:

CWU
150 The Broadway, Wimbledon SW19 1RX
Tel: 0208 9717 200; Fax: 020 8971 7300; e-mail: info@cwu.org;
website: www.cwu.org

The General Federation of Trade Unions can be contacted at:

GFTU Educational Trusts
Central House, Upper Woburn Place, London WC1H 0HY
Tel: 0207 387 2578; Fax: 0207 383 0820; e-mail: gftuhq@gftu.org.uk;
website: www.gftu.org.uk

The GMB can be contacted at:

GMB National Office
22/24 Worpole Road, London SW19 4DD
Tel: 020 8947 3131; Fax: 020 8944 6552; e-mail: info@gmb.org.uk;
website: www.gmb.org.uk

The National Union of Rail, Maritime and Transport Workers can be contacted at:

RMT
Unity House, 39 Chalton Street, London NW1 1JD
Tel: 020 7387 4771; Fax: 020 7387 4123; e-mail: info@rmt.org.uk;
website: www.rmt.org.uk

The Union of Construction, Allied Trades and Technicians can be contacted at:

UCATT General Office
177 Abbeville Road, London SW4 9RL
Tel: 0207 622 2442; Fax: 0207 720 4081; e-mail: info@ucatt.org.uk;
website: www.ucatt.info

Unison can be contacted at:

Unison Learning and Organizing Services
1 Mabledon Place, London WC1H 9AJ
Tel: 0845 355 0845; Fax: 0207 535 2105; e-mail: use contact form on
website: www.unison.org.uk

Unite can be contacted at:

Unite Education Department
Hayes Court, West Common Road, Hayes, Bromley BR2 7AU
Tel: 020 8462 7755; Fax: 020 8315 8234;
e-mail: education@unitetheunion.com;
website: www.unitetheunion.org.uk

Adult residential colleges

Adult residential colleges specialise in offering both short and long term courses for adults in a supportive, residential environment. The six adult residential colleges are:

Coleg Harlech
Harlech, Gwnedd LL46 2PU
Tel: 01766 781 900; Fax: 01766 817 621; e-mail: use enquiry form on website: www.harlech.ac.uk

Fircroft College
1018 Bristol Road, Selly Oak, Birmingham B29 6LH
Tel: 01214 720 116; Fax: 01214 725 481; e-mail: use contact form on website: www.fircroft.ac.uk

Hillcroft College (for women)
South Bank, Surbiton, Surrey KT6 6DF
Tel: 020 8399 2688; Fax: 020 8390 9171; e-mail: use enquiry form on website: www.hillcroft.ac.uk

Newbattle Abbey College
Dalkeith, Midlothian EH22 3LL
Tel: 0131 663 1921; Fax: 0131 654 0598;
e-mail: office@newbattleabbeycollege.ac.uk;
website: www.newbattleabbeycollege.ac.uk

Northern College
Wentworth Castle, Stainborough, Barnsley, South Yorkshire S75 3ET
Tel: 01226 776 000; Fax: 01226 776 025;
e-mail: courses@northern.ac.uk; website: www.northern.ac.uk

Ruskin College
Walton Street, Oxford OX1 2HE
Tel: 01865 554 331; Fax: 01865 554 372;
e-mail: enquiries@ruskin.ac.uk; website: www.ruskin.ac.uk

University applications

If you are interested in finding out more about courses offered by the Open University, you can contact them at the following address:

Student Registration & Enquiry Service
The Open University, PO Box 197, Milton Keynes MK7 6BJ
Tel: 0845 300 60 90; e-mail: general-enquiries@open.ac.uk;
website: www.open.ac.uk

If you want more information about applying for full-time courses at university in the United Kingdom, contact UCAS:

UCAS
Customer Service Unit, PO Box 28, Cheltenham GL52 3LZ
Tel: 0871 468 0 468; e-mail: enquiries@ucas.ac.uk;
website: www.ucas.com

Information for people with disabilities

If you are interested in finding out more about the residential training programme for people with disabilities, you can obtain more information from the Residential Training Unit:

Residential Training Unit
Government Office for the North East, Citygate, Gallowgate,
Newcastle upon Tyne NE1 4WH
Tel: 0191 202 3579; Fax: 0191 202 3626; e-mail: rtu@gone.gsi.gov.uk

Skill is a national charity that promotes opportunities for young people and adults with any kind of impairment in post-16 education, training and employment. It has published a booklet called *Disabled Students' Allowances* which gives guidance on the evidence needed from applicants.

Skill: the National Bureau for Students with Disabilities
Chapter House, 18–20 Crucifix Lane, London SE1 3JW
Tel: 0800 328 5050 Textphone: 0800 068 2422;
e-mail: info@skill.org.uk; website: www.skill.org.uk

Useful websites

Information and advice for young people

www.connexions-direct.com

This is the website of Connexions Direct, which provides information and advice for people aged 13–19. You can find contact details of your local Connexions service, where staff will be able to provide information about vacancies in your area. Information about Apprenticeships, Entry to Employment and sources of funding for further study can be found on this website.

Careers advice for adults

http://careersadvice.direct.gov.uk

This website provides useful information about all aspects of jobs, careers and learning. You can use the tools available on this site to assess your skills and interests and help you to produce a CV that can be used when you apply for Apprenticeships or jobs. There is a useful discussion group that includes information about Apprenticeships, careers, job-hunting and salaries.

www.careers-scotland.org.uk

This is the website of Careers Scotland, which is part of Skills Development Scotland, Scotland's new skills body. On this site you can access contact details of your local Careers Scotland agency. You can also find information about Modern Apprenticeships, careers, job-hunting, producing CVs and attending interviews. You can access links to other sites containing information more specific to the area in which you live.

www.planitplus.net

This website has been developed to help people of all ages to find out about career and learning opportunities in Scotland. It has information on over 600 job profiles, which is useful if you want to find out more about specific jobs that may be available.

www.careerswales.com

Careers Wales is funded by the Welsh Assembly Government and is available to give free careers information, advice and guidance to people of all ages in Wales. You can use the database on this site to hunt for an Apprenticeship or job in your area. Information is provided about the type of work that will be expected, the qualifications required and the wage you can expect to receive, along with contact details of the organisation offering the Apprenticeship or job. The service is available in English and Welsh.

www.careersserviceni.com
The Careers Service Northern Ireland has been developed to offer advice and guidance on learning, training and employment opportunities in Northern Ireland. The website contains contact details of careers services throughout Northern Ireland, along with comprehensive advice about writing a CV and covering letter. There are also useful tips about filling in application forms and attending a job interview.

www.tda.gov.uk
This is the website for the Training and Development Agency for Schools. On this site you can find out more information about employment-based training for schools. You can register to receive information and advice about funding and other financial aspects of becoming a teacher, as well as regular news and updates about teaching and teacher training.

Learning advice for adults

www.salp.org.uk
This is the website of Scotland's Learning Partnership (SLP), which is a national partnership of adult learners and providers in Scotland. The partnership has been set up to help encourage people to take part in adult and family learning. On this website you can obtain more information about the partnership and subscribe to the newsletter, which provides details of adult learning campaigns, projects and schemes available in Scotland.

Work-based learning information and advice

http://inourhands.lsc.gov.uk
Visit the 'learners' section of this website to obtain more information about learning new skills and gaining qualifications. There are some interesting case studies to read and useful links to other relevant sites. Your employer can access the 'employers' section for more information about how improving the skills and training of employees can help the business.

www.learningthroughwork.org

This website provides all the information you need about the Learning through Work scheme, including information about how the scheme works, eligibility criteria and available subject areas. You can make an online application through this website and use the online contact form to request more information.

www.apprenticeships.org.uk

This website contains all the information you need about Apprenticeships in England and has sections available for parents, employers and apprentices. You can use the online search facility to find a vacancy in your area and you can register an interest to receive more information about what is available. You can fill in the online form in the 'contact us' section of the website to receive a free DVD about Apprenticeships.

www.scottish-enterprise.com/modern-apprenticeships

This site provides information about Modern Apprenticeships in Scotland. Click on the area of the map in which you live to be directed to the relevant information.

www.jtltraining.com

JTL was formed in 1989 by the Electrical Contractors' Association (ECA) and the Electrical Electronic and Plumbing Union (now Unite, the Union) to manage training in the electrical sector. JTL is a leading training provider to the building services engineering sectors, supporting up to 9,700 Apprenticeships in England and Wales.

On the website you can find useful information about the different types of Apprenticeship available in this sector, such as electrical, plumbing, heating and ventilation and engineering maintenance. The website helps you to understand whether this type of Apprenticeship is the right choice for you, and if so, you can download an application pack.

www.euskills.co.uk

This is the website of Energy and Utility Skills, which is the Sector Skills Council for the electricity, gas, waste management and water industries. Although Energy and Utility Skills does not recruit apprentices it can provide you with useful information and advice about Apprenticeships within these industries. This includes useful links to employers who provide the jobs. There are sections on the website for people from all parts of the United Kingdom.

www.mappit.org.uk

This website contains detailed information about Modern Apprentice-ships in Scotland. You can access an alphabetical database by job type of all the Modern Apprenticeships that are available, or that may become available in the future. Contact details for each position are provided, along with information about the type of job, what work you will be expected to do, the wage you will be paid and the type of qualifications you will gain. You can also access information about the personal quali-ties required for the position and the progression routes you can expect upon completion.

www.delni.gov.uk/apprenticeshipsni

This is the website of the Department for Employment and Learning in Northern Ireland. On this site you can find more information about Appren-ticeships, with different sections available for apprentices, employers and training suppliers. You can access a map of Apprenticeship suppliers and download Level 2 and Level 3 Apprenticeships Frameworks. These provide detailed information about what is included in each Apprenticeship.

www.nidirect.gov.uk

This is the official government information website for Northern Ireland citizens. Click on the 'education, learning and skills' section, followed by the 'options after 16' section, which will direct you to the various learning and earning schemes that are available in Northern Ireland. This website also contains useful information about obtaining money for your studies, improving your work skills and Apprenticeships.

www.etcni.org.uk

The Engineering Training Council (ETC) is an employer-led body, governed by a council whose members are elected to ensure a broad representation of the engineering community in Northern Ireland. It is dedicated to supporting the engineering industry by coordinating training and learning opportunities for new entrants and the existing workforce. On the website you can find further information about the Engineering Apprenticeships that are available, including lists of employers, job descriptions and the skills and qualifications that are required. You can download an application pack or fill in the online form if you are interested in applying for an Apprenticeship.

Training and skills advice for businesses

www.traintogain.gov.uk

Train to Gain is a government national skills service that supports employers of all sizes in all sectors by offering advice about improving business performance through training. This website contains all the information employers need to know about the Train to Gain scheme. You can find out how the scheme is organised and read about eligibility criteria and possible sources of funding. There is a contact form available for employers who wish to get in touch with a skills broker.

www.businesslink.gov.uk

Practical advice for businesses is available on this website, including information about finance and grants, employing people and growing your business. You can access a training directory with a link to work-related training courses on the learndirect business website (www.learndirect.co.uk/businessinfo). You can also obtain contact details of your local Business Link service by using the postcode search facility on this website.

www.lds4b.com

This is the learndirect Scotland for business site that provides details of support schemes available for businesses in Scotland. The site contains useful fact sheets about what is available, a course search of over 18,000 courses and training workbooks to download. You can ring the helpline for advice or to make an appointment with your local training provider on 08456 000 111.

http://wales.gov.uk

Visit this site and click on the 'education and skills' section, followed by the 'information for employers' section for information and advice for businesses in Wales. Guides are divided into three categories: information for businesses new to training; information for businesses needing to get better training; and information for larger organisations seeking skills excellence. More information about the schemes available can be obtained by calling 0845 60 661 60 or by e-mailing info@skillspeoplesuccess.com.

www.delni.gov.uk

Visit this site and click on the 'skills and training' section to access information about the training opportunities available for businesses in Northern Ireland. You can find more information about Essential Skills training and Management Analysis and Planning (MAP), which enables your organisation, with the assistance of a business consultant, to complete an online assessment of its management and leadership development needs.

www10.employersguide.org.uk

This website provides an employer's guide to training. You can access this service to search for a training provider in your area. The database can be searched by keyword and postcode. The search results provide information about the type of course, duration, attendance and the qualifications that can be achieved.

www.investorsinpeople.co.uk

This website contains all you need to know about Investors in People. You can click on the map to find the contact details of your nearest Investors in People Centre. Here staff will be able to offer advice about how a company can achieve Investors in People status and illustrate the benefits that can be gained from working towards the standard.

Information and advice for jobseekers

www.jobcentreplus.gov.uk

Jobcentre Plus is a government agency that is part of the Department for Work and Pensions (DWP). Its role is to support people of working age from welfare into work and to help fill vacancies advertised by employers. You can use the postcode search facility on the website to find the contact details of your nearest Jobcentre Plus office.

www.remploy.co.uk

Remploy is one of the United Kingdom's leading providers of employment services and employment to people with disabilities. Remploy has a network of town and city centre branches that are available to offer support and advice to people with disabilities. Contact details can be obtained from the website, along with information about the services offered to people who are out of work and claiming disability, sickness or incapacity benefits.

http://nextstep.direct.gov.uk
Nextstep is a free service that offers face-to-face help and support about training, learning and employment. You can use the nextstep service if you are aged 20 or over, or aged 18 or 19 and have been referred to next-step by Jobcentre Plus. On this site you can obtain contact details of your nearest nextstep office.

http://jobseekers.direct.gov.uk
You can search for jobs, training careers, childcare and voluntary work on this site. You can search by job type and geographical location. Each entry contains a description of the job, wages, working hours, date posted, pension details, application procedures and employer contact details.

www.jobcentreonline.com
If you live in Northern Ireland you can use this site to find job vacancies in your area.

www.delni.gov.uk/trainingforsuccess
This section of the Department for Employment and Learning website contains information about the Training for Success scheme in Northern Ireland. This is a scheme available to help people aged 16–18 obtain employment. There is a section for young people, employers and training suppliers. Contact details of all the relevant training suppliers can be obtained by clicking on the relevant entry in the table displayed.

www.adviceguide.org.uk
This is the information and advice website of the Citizens Advice Bureau. Visit the relevant part of the site for your country to obtain information about benefits and job grants when you start work.

Trade union learning and funding advice

www.unionlearn.org.uk
This website has been established by the Trade Union Congress (TUC) to help unions to become learning organisations and spread the life-long learning message. On this site you can access the 'unionlearn' learning and careers advice service, which is a free, impartial and confidential service that helps people to develop new skills, improve

their job prospects or change jobs. You can use the database to search more than 950,000 courses or obtain free expert advice by calling 08000 92 91 90.

www.skills4schools.org.uk

This website has been set up by Unison to offer advice and guidance for school support staff. It provides information about personal development and career pathways, helping you to decide which course might be right for you, and information about overcoming common barriers to learning.

Funding for learning

www.hkf.org.uk

This is the website of the Helena Kennedy Foundation, which is an organisation that supports disadvantaged students who have overcome significant barriers in order to continue with their education at university level. It contains information about its bursaries and mentoring programme and provides details of the eligibility criteria for the bursaries.

http://ema.direct.gov.uk

This is the government EMA website. Here you can find more information about the EMA, including the eligibility criteria and application process. This site also links to the government information website (www.direct. gov.uk), which contains more information about EMAs.

www.emascotland.com

This is the EMA Scotland website, which provides all the information you need to know about the EMA in Scotland. There is a section for administrators, current students and new students. You can download a sample learning agreement from this site and access contact details of colleges and local councils in Scotland.

www.studentfinancewales.co.uk

This is the website of Student Finance Wales. Visit the EMA/ALG micro site to find more information about the EMA in Wales. (The ALG is an Assembly Learning Grant of up to £1,500, paid to students from low income families who are aged 19 or over, whereas the EMA is a fortnightly allowance paid to students from low income households aged 16–18.)

You can e-mail the EMA Wales Customer Services Team at EMAWALES@ slc.co.uk for more information.

www.delni.gov.uk

This is the website of the Department for Employment and Learning in Northern Ireland. Type 'EMA' into the search box to be directed to the information you require about the EMA in Northern Ireland. Application forms and guidance notes can be downloaded from this site. You can also access useful information about other sources of funding for study in Northern Ireland.

www.ilawales.co.uk

Visit this site for information about Individual Learning Accounts in Wales. It provides information about the ILA, eligibility criteria and application procedures. There is also some useful information on the benefits to be gained from returning to learning and you can download a publication called a *Guide to Funding* from this site.

www.ilascotland.org.uk

Visit this site for more information about Individual Learning Accounts in Scotland. The site contains all the information you need about the ILA, including eligibility criteria and a useful course search that enables you to search for a course by subject in your location. You can download an application pack for an ILA from the website.

www.cityandguilds.com

This is the City & Guilds website, with a section for people in the United Kingdom and another for people in the rest of the world. You can find out more information about the type of qualifications that are available and the subject areas that are on offer. The 'financial assistance' page provides more information about the access bursary and you can download an application form from this page.

www.student-support-saas.gov.uk

This is the website of the Student Awards Agency for Scotland, which is the organisation that deals with student financial support in Scotland. More information about all aspects of funding for further and higher education, including childcare, in Scotland can be obtained from this site.

https://skillsaccounts.direct.gov.uk
Skills Accounts have been piloted in England in 2009 and it is hoped that they will soon be available to everyone over the age of 19 throughout England. Skills Accounts offer advice about sources of support to help you with your learning and provide course information, so that you can under-stand the options available to you when deciding about your skills and career. Currently 'skills vouchers' are being piloted as part of this scheme in the East Midlands and South East regions of England. These show what funding may be available for your chosen course. Visit this website for more information about the scheme and to register your details.

Contact details for schools and colleges

www.getoncourse.org
This is the website for the Association of Northern Ireland Colleges. Visit this site to link to all six further education colleges in Northern Ireland.

www.ascol.org.uk
This is the website of the Association of Scotland's Colleges. Visit this site to obtain contact details of all of Scotland's FE colleges.

www.aoc.co.uk
This is the website of the Association of Colleges website. If you live in England or Wales visit this site to obtain contact details of your local FE college.

www.independentschools.com
This site enables you to use the postcode locator to find an independent school in your area, including sixth form schools and colleges.

www.arca.uk.net
This is the website of the Adult Residential Colleges Association. Visit this site to find out more about adult residential colleges and the courses on offer. There is a map showing the location of all colleges in the United Kingdom and you can click on the relevant college to be directed to its website.

www.wea.org.uk
The Workers' Educational Association (WEA) is non-party-political and works closely with a range of partners including local authorities, universities and

other voluntary and community organisations. Courses are organised by over 600 local branches throughout the United Kingdom. To find a WEA course near to you, use the postcode locator available on the website.

www.odlqc.org.uk
This is the website of the Open and Distance Learning Quality Council. It contains useful advice about choosing a course, costs and what to do if things go wrong. It also lists, and provides contact details of, all accredited distance learning providers.

University courses and applications

www.findfoundationdegree.co.uk
More information about foundation degrees can be obtained from this site, and there is a useful course search facility to help you find a foundation degree course that is suitable for your needs. You can search by category (which gives you a broad listing of courses available), or you can search by region and/or course title. The site also contains useful information for employers and course providers.

www.ucas.com
UCAS is the organisation responsible for managing applications to full-time higher education courses in the United Kingdom. Visit this site to find out more about the application procedure and to use the course search facility to find a university course. The site also contains useful information aimed at parents, mature students and disabled students, along with comprehensive information about student finance.

Student employment services

www.nases.org.uk
The National Association of Student Employment Services (NASES) is the national representative body for practitioners of all styles of student employment services. On the NASES website you can find an alphabetical list of student employment services in universities throughout the country. The website contains information leaflets covering issues such as applying for jobs, income tax and National Insurance.

Gap years, placements and sponsorship

www.work-experience.org
This is the website of the National Council for Work Experience (NCWE), which promotes, supports and develops work experience for the benefit of students, organisations and the economy. On this site you can read work placement case studies and access links to organisations offering work placements for students. You can also find out about the Quality Mark, which is an accreditation awarded by the NCWE to recognise employers that have reached the required standard of work experience provision.

www.prospects.ac.uk
Prospects is an organisation that provides careers advice for graduate students. On this website you can find information about a variety of organisations that offer year-long work placements, vacation placements, summer internships and trainee opportunities. You can also find information about producing CVs, attending job interviews and increasing your chances of success.

www.work-placement.co.uk
This site contains useful information about work placements, including details of the National Work Placement Exhibitions that take place in London and Birmingham. There is also some useful careers advice on this site.

www.itraineeship.com
This website seeks to match graduates with international employers. It provides detailed listings of a variety of international employers, work and placement opportunities, including short- and long-term contracts before, during and after your course.

www.targetjobs.co.uk
This website has a useful database that you can search for all kinds of jobs, including short-term jobs for work experience. You can search the database by sector, keyword and region.

www.topinternships.com
This website provides information on internships and placements for UK undergraduates. You can search the database by sector, discipline, date,

location and keyword. You will need to register to view the results of your search.

www.everythingyouwantedtoknow.com

Visit the 'job/placement' section of this site to find out about sponsorship, placements and graduate opportunities.

www.scholarship-search.org.uk

Visit the 'sponsorship' section of the Hot Courses website to find out what opportunities are available. The listings provide details of the amount of sponsorship, duration, application opening and closing dates, number of awards and subject areas. There is also a link to the relevant sponsor's website.

Student discounts

www.nussl.co.uk

This is the website of NUS Services, which is owned by students' unions and the NUS. Its mission is to 'create, develop and sustain competitive advantages for member Students' Unions – reducing costs and maximising commercial revenues'. Through NUS Services, students' unions can obtain goods and marketing services at reduced prices and savings can be passed onto students.

www.nus.org.uk

The NUS is a voluntary membership organisation that represents the interests of students across the United Kingdom. You can obtain a wide range of information about all aspects of university life from the NUS, including information about the discounts that you could receive as a student. You can purchase an NUS Extra card from this site, which enables you to receive a wide variety of discounts on goods and services throughout the United Kingdom.

Self-employment and entrepreneurship

www.princes-trust.org.uk

If you are aged between 18 and 30 and have a business idea, the Prince's Trust may be able to help with advice and funding. This website contains information about the type of help and support that may be available.

Information about qualifications

www.qcda.gov.uk

This is the website of the Qualifications and Curriculum Development Agency (QCDA), which is a new organisation that is to be developed from the Qualifications and Curriculum Authority. Here you can find more information about all aspects of 14–19 education and training, Apprenticeships, GCSEs, NVQs, A levels, diplomas, work-related learning and the qualifications and credit framework.

www.sqa.org.uk

This is the website of the Scottish Qualifications Authority, which is the national body in Scotland responsible for the development, accreditation, assessment and certification of qualifications other than degrees. Here you can find further information about SVQs, Modern Apprenticeships and other types of education and training in Scotland.

www.edexcel.com

This is the website of Edexcel, which is the awarding body of BTEC qualifications. On this site there is a section for students, which includes information about the qualifications that you can work towards. There is also some useful information on study options in the United Kingdom and overseas, along with some tips on taking and passing examinations. You can use the BTEC National Centre Finder to locate schools and colleges offering BTEC Nationals.

www.ocrnationals.com

This is the website of the awarding body for OCR Nationals. On this site you can find more information about the different levels of qualification and read case studies about people who have completed their OCR Nationals. You can also access the 'career path finder' that enables you to match careers with your OCR qualifications.

www.qaa.ac.uk

This is the website of the Quality Assurance Agency for Higher Education. On this site you can find out more information about higher education qualifications and the Framework for Higher Education Qualifications (FHEQ), which applies to England, Wales and Northern Ireland.

Credit frameworks for learners and suppliers

www.nuccat.ac.uk

This is the website of the Northern Universities Consortium for Credit Accumulation and Transfer (NUCCAT), which is a federation of some 40 higher education institutions in the United Kingdom. On the website you can find more information about work-related learning and credits in higher education.

www.nicats.ac.uk

This is the website of the Northern Ireland Credit Accumulation and Transfer System (NICATS), which is a credit framework for valuing, describing, measuring and recognising all learning. More information about this system, including a useful FAQ section, can be obtained from this site.

www.hefcw.ac.uk

This is the website of the Higher Education Funding Council for Wales. If you want to know more about achieving credits at university in Wales, enter 'Credit and Qualifications Framework for Wales (CQFW)' to be directed to the relevant section of this website.

www.seec.org.uk

This is the website of the Southern England Consortium for Credit Accumulation and Transfer. SEEC is a registered charity that was formed in 1985. It was the first higher education consortium for credit accumulation and transfer (CATS) in the United Kingdom. On this site you can find more information about credits in higher education, and information about accrediting your prior learning.

www.scqf.org.uk

This is the website of the Scottish Credit and Qualifications Framework, which promotes lifelong learning in Scotland and enables people of all ages and circumstances to access education and training. On the website you can find useful information about returning to education and read case studies from adult learners. You can also find out about the different levels of qualification and information about the number of credits awarded for each of them.

Index

Index of Advertisers